AF316661

The Other Life of Abraham Lincoln's Barber

The Other Life of Abraham Lincoln's Barber

William G Herbert

ISBN: 9798218478339

First Printing, 2024

To
Margaret Louise Lucinda Johnson Herbert
1910 - 1954
Giver of Life and Inspiration

Also by William G. Herbert

A Place Near the Front is the story of how the author's immigrant father earns his US citizenship as part of an all-black US Army unit that fights heroically in the trenches of World War One France to preserve the freedoms of Europeans that they, themselves do not enjoy in America. They battle not only the German Army, but their own commanders who resent black troops. (2016)

The Bones of Louverture is set in the turbulent period following the 1987 overthrow of Haitian dictator, Jean-Claude "Baby-Doc" Duvalier. It tells of the descent of two street protesters into a world of drugs and crime, and of a subsequent redemption, after the two veer from their mission of helping the troubled nation achieve the promise of its heroic slave-revolt founding. (2022)

CONTENTS

Because a story is a story, you may tell it as your imagination and your being and your environment dictate.

Nelson Mandela

Historic accomplishments and extraordinary actions often go unnoticed when they are the achievements of those who are not well-known public figures. For this reason, many exceptional people are not fully appreciated in their own lifetimes. Their contributions are often quickly forgotten, forever unknown even to their own descendants unless by some happenchance, their work somehow comes to light and is appreciated at some future date.

Within this harsh reality, most of us, both the exceptional and the ordinary, are likely no more than three or four generations away from total oblivion. That is unless conscious steps are taken to record our significant actions and their impact on society.

Because dominant cultures are so often unwilling to acknowledge the contributions of all segments of society, the issue is particularly relevant within the context of black history, both in family settings and larger geo-political arenas. It is in this spirit that I endeavor to tell the extraordinary life story of my great-grandfather, Solomon James Johnson.

Born free in 1844 and known to family and friends as "Sweet" Johnson, Solomon began a career of service as a Civil War Union soldier and White House presidential guard. Adhering to the multitasking expected of a black man who sought advancement in that era, he also served as Abraham Lincoln's personal barber. In a most unusual journey, he went on to become the first black clerk in the US Federal Government and a leader in the early days of black Masonry in America.

Because of his association with a revered US president, his prolific letter writing, the volume of letters and newspaper stories written about him, and a family oral history passed down through many generations, much is known about Solomon. To write this book, that knowledge was augmented with facts and data gleaned from census records, city directories, Masonic literature, and government correspondence that includes letters about Solomon written and signed by Lincoln himself. But even with all that is known about Solomon, there are missing details, as is usually the case with the passing of those who are not widely known personalities or public figures.

My goal in writing this book was not to create a fully cited dissertation that would necessarily contain gaps where source data is incomplete. Instead, I wanted to tell Solomon's life story in a way that captures his essence and historical significance. To the extent possible, I based this narrative on known facts and historical events. But where that was impossible, I took the liberty of reconstructing missing pieces with reasonable assumptions and best guesses to provide "connective tissue" that bridges gaps between known historical events.

Although this approach may not tightly adhere to the rules of academic research, I believe it has enabled me to better tell Solomon's compelling story and maintain the flow of his journey, than would have been possible with a rigorously accurate but perhaps somewhat dry research paper that lacked important detail. In the interest of literary integrity, I have therefore categorized this accounting of Solomon's life as a work of historical fiction, not biography or narrative non-fiction, even though most of what I have written is fact-based.

To fully describe the experiences and challenges faced by Solomon and other black people of his era, I found it necessary to comment on a broad range of issues and personalities that shaped antebellum America. To some, it might seem that addressing such a wide scope of topics might cause the narrative to expand into matters not directly relevant to

Solomon's life. But any attempt to paint a picture of Solomon in terms of his personal experiences only would not tell the full story of how much his life was shaped by the momentous events and key influencers of the time. Thus, in writing this book, I tell not only of the people and events of Solomon's daily life but also those of the broader environment that shaped him.

For example, though Solomon never met or personally interacted with Frederick Douglass, the fiery black leader was an important public figure of the era. Because he served a key role in the evolution of the racial attitudes of Abraham Lincoln, who was not only the Great Emancipator, but also a key figure in Solomon's life, it was necessary for Douglass to be a part of Solomon's story. Similar attention had to be paid to a broad spectrum of other issues ranging from the dreaded practice of "slave-breaking" to the political drama and turmoil surrounding Reconstruction.

I feel it necessary to comment on my choice and use of racial terminology. Segments of the book that describe events in Civil War era real-time include such racial references as Negro, colored, and black, each with implied value connotations of the time. Other book segments presented from the perspective of a present-day narrator engaging in historical storytelling and commentary use more currently appropriate terminology. The terms Negro and colored, widely accepted by all races as inoffensive in 1865, are now thought of as outdated or derogatory. Similarly, the designation, black, now celebrated by most as a prideful and honorable label, was deemed insulting and demeaning by many people of color during Solomon's lifetime. It is hoped that the reader will appreciate the challenge and delicate balance involved in employing modern sensibilities to tell a story involving controversial language and terminology of past, racially troubled times. Complicating the situation is the unfortunate reality that much of the racial intolerance of the antebellum era persists today.

Finally, it would have been impossible to complete this book without the support, assistance and independent research that came from several important sources. More than fifty years ago, an outstanding geneal-ogist and historian, the late Paul Sluby began digging into my great-grandfather's history. His exceptional research led to the creation of a Permanent Digital Exhibit (10-1-2015) at Howard University's Moor-land-Spingarn Research Center. My conversations with Dr. Sluby and the fine staff at the research center were invaluable in the completion of this project. Other important support came from my daughter Yolande Herbert who first informed me of the existence of the digital exhibit and who later provided important insights and perspectives as a beta-reader of my final manuscript. Two other beta-readers who provided invalu-able inspiration, feedback and suggestions were my great friends and fel-low members of the esteemed Detroit literary group *Brothers Also Read*, the late Cornell Mays and his brother Dexter Mays.

Missing

History is not everything, but it is a starting point. History is a clock that people use to tell their political and cultural time of the day. It is a compass they use to find themselves on the map of human geography. It tells them where they are but, more importantly, what they must be.

John Henrick Clark

In the summer of 1859, three months after young Solomon began barber training, three black boys disappeared from the streets of Columbus, Ohio. Fifteen-year-old Solomon knew the boys well, as their families had all migrated from Virginia and settled in the same Columbus neighborhood at the same time. When missing posters throughout the city generated no responses, everyone suspected the boys might have fallen victim to child-snatchers who kidnapped black children in free states and sold them to plantation owners in the South. If abducted, the boys would likely spend the rest of their lives as someone's property in a distant state, never to see their families again.

At the time, gangs known as *Blackbirders* operated widely throughout the North by luring or violently seizing free blacks and escaped bondsmen. Alcohol was a favorite means of compromising black men who normally would avoid solicitations from white strangers and rarely venture into unfamiliar surroundings. Kidnappers often targeted children who could be tempted with candy or fruit. Unable to fight off stronger adults, many children were unable to recognize situations in which they were vulnerable to abduction. Kidnappers made off with their victims by setting up chains of stations similar to those moving escaped slaves from the South. These networks were known as *The Reverse Underground Railroad*.

The missing boys were never seen again. Although Columbus had always been one of several northern population centers seen as symbols of hope for freedom seekers migrating from the slaveholding South, throughout the city there were now lingering fears of abduction by rogue slave catchers.

As Solomon walked home to *Hanson's*, his father's front-porch barber shop, one afternoon six months after the disappearance of the three boys, a passing black stranger asked him whether he would like to earn some extra change by unloading cargo from a ship tied up at the Scioto River docks. Solomon responded to the light-skinned transient that he was already working and not interested. A few days later, he saw the same man talking to Paul, a black youngster who shined shoes at Hanson's. Solomon didn't give much thought to their discussion, but an alarm went off for him when Paul didn't show up for work the next morning, as the young bootblack was a child of the streets who never missed a day of work. The barber shop was the closest thing to a family Paul had ever had. Later that same day, Solomon heard that two other boys from the neighborhood were also missing.

It hadn't occurred to Solomon that the well-behaved and courteous young stranger might be seeking victims for abduction. He had always assumed that kidnappers were roughneck trash who did their mischief with nighttime violence, not friendly afternoon banter. But the more he thought about it, the more his suspicions made sense. Most black people, especially children, would be less wary of an engaging young black man than a white stranger. They might be inclined to take him up on what seemed to be a harmless offer of work and an opportunity to pick up some pocket money. It sickened Solomon to think that a black man would sink so low as to entrap and sell a black child into slavery. It was especially troubling that the dark-skinned youngster had been victimized by someone with mixed-race features and coloring. The incident brought into focus the bizarre and troubling aspect of America's racial dysfunction that seemed to entitle the mixed-race offspring produced by the nation's original sin to look down upon and abuse their darker-hued brethren.

Angry with himself that he had misread a dangerous situation, Solomon assembled a small rescue party consisting of himself, two neighborhood friends, and the other shop bootblack. They armed themselves with straight razors and clubs and prepared to head for the dock even though they still weren't sure that Paul had been kidnapped, or to which boat he might have been taken. But Solomon felt they had to act quickly. If Paul had really been snatched, his abductors would likely waste no time getting him out of town.

Solomon's father was servicing a customer but noticed his son's animated discussion with the three other teenagers on the street in front of the shop. "What's the problem, gents?" Hanson inquired of the boys after momentarily excusing himself from his customer.

"Paul is missing, and I think he's been kidnapped," Solomon anxiously shot back. "And I believe the guy who took him tried to snare me yesterday with a story about some work at the dock. Paul is always broke, so it's likely he'd be anxious to pick up some pocket money."

"You're probably right," Hanson responded, "but I don't want you fellows going to the docks by yourself. It's dangerous down there, even at this time of the morning. I suggest you head down to the Marshall's office and get him involved. The chances of Paul being rescued are more likely with the Marshall leading the way than with you and your companions getting into a dispute with kidnappers who are probably well-armed."

Solomon immediately alerted the marshal. Less than one hour later, with Solomon and Hanson accompanying him, the lawman and several deputies proceeded to the dock and boarded the one commercial vessel remaining at the pier, a two-masted riverboat emblazoned with the name *Triton*. Solomon quickly identified the stranger who had attempted to lure him to the ship, and after a thorough search, Paul and two other boys were discovered. They had been bound, gagged, and locked in a small compartment below deck. Beaten and forced to drink alcohol to make them drowsy and quiet, the boys were convinced they would never again see home. The marshal arrested the kidnapper and the ship's captain and impounded the boat.

News of the rescue quickly spread around town. Solomon enjoyed a bit of celebrity and was repeatedly requested to tell of the abduction and rescue. The unusual episode made for good barbershop storytelling.

***

Despite the ever-present danger of kidnapping, early 1800s Columbus was one of the most popular Northern cities for free black people to settle. Thought to be a fairly safe distance from the Southern slave catchers sent North to retrieve escaped slaves, many fugitives from bondage arrived in Columbus as Underground Railroad (UGRR) passengers. Others came as freedmen, in some cases attracted by local opportunities, and in others, sent to Ohio by slave masters who had emancipated them.

The Central Ohio city had been founded in 1812 on the east side of the Scioto River and later became the capital of Ohio. The federal census two years earlier had counted residents in the newly formed Franklin County and recorded forty-three "free colored people," approximately one percent of the county's population. But that number only included those who did not fear being counted by a US marshal, the authority responsible for enforcing the 1793 Fugitive Slave Act, a national law mandating that, upon capture, all escaped slaves be returned to their masters. The law also required full cooperation of officials and citizens in free states to which slaves had fled.

By the time Columbus was formally incorporated as a city on March 3, 1824, it had some five thousand residents. By 1840, the population had grown to just over six thousand, almost ten percent of it black. A significant portion of this growth could be traced to the city's strategic location as a stop on a major Underground Railroad line, one of the secretive networks that could help escaping slaves move along escape routes that were neither advertised nor written.

A free state situated between the slave states of Virginia and Kentucky, Ohio had more than 400 miles of border between free-state and slave-state. With only 250 miles from the Ohio River to Lake Erie and freedom to the north in Canada, Ohio's 3,000 miles of Underground Railroad routes were some of the most heavily traveled in the nation.

Born free in 1844, Solomon James Johnson was the seventh of nine children raised by Susannah and Hanson Johnson. Hanson had spent his early years in Virginia and moved to Columbus in 1823 where he began his home barbering business. As was the case for most black barbers of the era, his customers were mostly white. In his two-chair shop, he taught his six sons, Lucius, Allin, Richard, Douglas, Solomon, and John the trade. As a young man, Solomon was known to family, friends, and barbershop customers by the childhood nickname, "Sweet," an honorific he had righteously earned with his key role in the kidnap rescue. So widely was he known in the neighborhood by this name that the 1860 census identified him as "Sweet Johnson" instead of "Solomon Johnson."

Over the years, Hanson accumulated large land holdings, a most unusual situation at the time considering the limited opportunities for black men to build wealth. A prominent community leader, he was a major supporter and benefactor of Columbus's Bethel Church.

By 1850, Columbus appeared to be on the verge of becoming a major urban metropolis. Public support for community schools had increased, efforts toward higher education had begun, and public executions had been eliminated. City leaders had optimistically predicted that, because of the increase in local manufacturing and the expansion of railroads, the city's population would reach 50,000 by 1850. But, in 1859, with the nation headed toward a civil war, and the outmigration of many locals to growing population centers in other free states, not quite 19,000 citizens resided in the City of Columbus.

The changing face of slavery in America had created new forms of bondage. In the early 1800s, there were two million enslaved in the US, 99 percent of them in the South. White settlers arriving in new territories along the Gulf Coast had created an ongoing demand for slave labor to cut sugarcane and pick cotton. But options for obtaining slaves had been severely limited in 1808 when the U.S. Congress outlawed slave imports from Africa and the Caribbean. Their powers enhanced in 1852 by a new and far more draconian version of the Fugitive Slave Law, interstate slavecatchers filled some of the need. But since the number of recaptured slaves was small, slavecatchers expanded their focus to free people of color.

During slavery, freedmen were required to carry certificates of freedom and register with county courts. Ex-slaves had to carry their papers at all times to avoid being mistaken as slaves, captured and re-enslaved. Even those carrying their papers ran the risk of having them confiscated and destroyed by unscrupulous slavecatchers. Because of these oppressive conditions, the increase in Reverse Underground Railroad abductions like the *Triton* incident, and births among the enslaved, by the middle 1850s the US enslaved population had grown to four million.

Although both free black people and fugitive slaves were eager to leave slave states, they were not welcome in most Northern states. Ohio had outlawed slavery in the early 1800s but immediately began implementing laws to keep black people from entering the state and to control them if they got in. It enacted the first of its *Black Laws* in 1802. Similar laws were passed in other free states, but those implemented in Ohio were notorious throughout the US. It was often said that the slave states treated their free black population with less contempt and oppression than that inflicted by the free state of Ohio on its own citizens of color. Under these laws, black people were required to meet rigid qualifications to enter the state. They were barred from serving in the militia and not allowed to send their children to school. Even worse, they were unable to bear witness against whites and were not allowed to work unless they carried certificates of freedom. Commenting on the oppressive situation in his newspaper, the *North Star*, Frederick Douglass wrote:

> In no State of the Union are to be found laws more cruel, unjust and atrocious than those on the Statute Book of Ohio.

Black people in Ohio had continued to live cautiously and uncomfortably under these oppressive laws until abolition movements began stirring throughout the US. In the run-up to the Civil War, Ohio's Black Laws were finally repealed, and the Supreme Court of Ohio ruled that any slave brought into the state was immediately free.

Some Ohioans had come to believe that, with war imminent, conditions would improve for citizens of color. But the state's official attitude became clear when newspapers printed an alarming excerpt from the 1862 report of a state legislative committee that had been formed to investigate the wave of black immigration from slave states to Ohio:

> The Negro race is looked upon by the people of Ohio as a class to be kept by themselves; to be barred of social intercourse with whites; to be deprived of all advantages which they cannot enjoy in common with their own class.... The colored man will not in all future time that he may remain an inhabitant... attain any material improvement in the social and political rights over that which he now enjoys.

Despite these negative attitudes, the black population in Columbus continued to increase. The pressure of this in-migration, together with the scarcity of available housing, made it a profitable business to build and rent homes to these new arrivals. Hanson Johnson and other savvy black entrepreneurs converted this situation into a successful real estate strategy, one that would later come to be known as *blockbusting*. For the most part, whites bitterly resisted the movement of blacks into their neighborhoods and tried to keep them in segregated areas. Hanson quietly bought homes in Franklin County's Montgomery Township, a white neighborhood in the northern section of Downtown Columbus. He made his acquisitions through white real estate dealers who kept his race a secret until the sale was completed. Because of his color, he paid higher than market rate for these initial acquisitions. But he knew that as soon as he placed a black resident into the house, he would be able to buy nearby properties at reduced prices as panicky whites sold their properties at a loss rather than live near a person of color.

Time and again, Hanson would use this same strategy to increase his holdings. By the time Solomon executed his mission to rescue the missing boys, Hanson had already accumulated several choice parcels of land just one block north of the State Capitol Building and two blocks from City Hall. Throughout his career, Hanson would continue to build his real estate portfolio in the downtown neighborhood bounded by Third and Fourth Streets on the west and east, and by Long Street and Gay Street on the north and south.

Barbering was a particularly popular occupation for black men in the Ohio capitol. An integral part of the local political and business infrastructure, black barbers used shop small talk, gossip, and overheard customer conversations to glean information useful to them as conductors on the Underground Railroad that operated out of Columbus. Reverend James Poindexter, the first man of color elected to the Columbus City Council and the School Board was both a barber and a conductor on the Underground Railroad. Although his various positions gave him great influence in the black community, he had found little emancipation support among the roughly 50 percent of white Ohioans who were against slavery. Many of them believed they would have to wait for God to end the evil system of bondage.

By the time the Civil War began in 1861, Solomon had trained and become one of Columbus's top young barbers. Though still in his teens, he was one of several who had gained proficiency in the technique of dyeing white men's hair into the popular "senatorial silver." From time to time, he practiced his skills on the hair of captured Confederate officers who were permitted to temporarily leave the nearby Camp Chase prisoner barracks to visit his father's shop.

Black men in Ohio and elsewhere in the North had come to believe that if they volunteered to serve in the war, and aid the Union in a time of need, they could count on greater civil equality after the war, regardless of whether slavery was eliminated in the South. But in the initial months of the war, they were not allowed to serve as soldiers in what white Ohioans protectively labelled a "white man's fight." Attitudes suddenly changed, however, when it seemed likely that the city of Cincinnati might be attacked by Confederate troops from Kentucky. The city immediately called on the services of one thousand local black men who came to be known as the *Black Brigade*. In 1863, similar regiments of colored troops were organized in Massachusetts and Kansas. A prominent Ohio black merchant took the leadership in assembling nine hundred Ohioans of color for service with the Massachusetts 54th Volunteer Colored Infantry.

When the news of his successful kidnap rescue effort spread outside Columbus, nineteen-year-old Solomon was recruited by the 54th. He had been inspired to join the famed unit by newspaper coverage about the bravery of one of its members who had distinguished himself on the battlefield, not as a cook, stevedore, or any of the other kinds of jobs in which black servicemen usually found themselves trapped. William Harvey Carney had been promoted to sergeant for his heroism in the July 18, 1863, assault on Fort Wagner in South Carolina, actions which ultimately earned him the Medal of Honor.

Solomon was rejected by the 54th when he couldn't pass the physical. Although energetic, hard-working, and not afraid of a fight, throughout his life Solomon was plagued with a variety of physical ailments, principal among them consumption (later recognized as tuberculosis). Undaunted by his rejection from the Massachusetts Volunteers, Solomon was on hand, a few months later, for the formation of the Union Light Guard. Otherwise known as the Seventh Independent Company of Ohio Volunteer Cavalry, the unit was created by recruiting one cavalryman from each of Ohio's then existing counties. Some one hundred men in number, the Guard was assembled for "special service" under the direction of Ohio Governor David Tod in the fall of 1863. The nature of the special service was not disclosed until the unit was mustered into duty.

Although the military was strictly segregated, it was common practice at the time for white units to incorporate the services of a few black or Native American men who had special skills required by the unit. While needed skills usually involved kitchen or laborer work, they sometimes extended to other specialties such as scouting or spying. Those providing these services were not official members of the unit but were carried as part of the Quartermaster Reserve Corporation.

Ambitious and persuasive, Solomon convinced a top Light Guard commander, one of the customers at his father's shop, that he could serve double duty as both a Light Guardsman and a barber for the otherwise all-white unit. After three of his father's white customers vouched for his character, toughness, and excellent barbering skills, Solomon was added to the unit with a quartermaster designation. His parents were not happy to see him leave Columbus but supported his effort to be part of a righteous war effort to free the enslaved. Hanson, having left his own home state of Virginia to seek his fortune in Ohio, appreciated his son's need to strike out into new territories to make his own mark in the world.

Early in November of 1863, the Light Guard was ordered to Washington and informed by the Secretary of War that the special service for which it had been created was to serve as bodyguard and mounted escort for President Lincoln. The Light Guard would share those duties with the 150th Pennsylvania Infantry. For the most part an admirer of the president, Solomon was pleased to learn of his assignment. But other members of the unit were bitterly disappointed at what they anticipated would be a service of "glorious inactivity." Some, with outside support, worked hard to have the Light Guard reassigned to duty at the front where it could share in battlefield action. Later, however, as Lincoln's reputation as a wartime president grew, the unit came to appreciate the honor of having been chosen as personal escort and bodyguard of a man they now recognized as one of America's great leaders.

The White House

Our minds are made up to live here if we can, or die here if we must; so, every attempt to remove us, will be, as it ought to be, labor lost. Here we are, and here we shall remain. While our brethren are in bondage on these shores; it is idle to think of inducing any considerable number of the free colored people to quit this for a foreign land.

Frederick Douglass

Upon arrival in Washington, the Union Light Guard, one-hundred-eight men strong, was billeted on the White House grounds, just south of the Treasury Department building on the west side of 15th Street, facing D and F Streets. The unit's horses were stabled in an area that would later become the site of Albaugh's Opera House. The White House grounds consisted of the Treasury Building, the White House itself, and to its west, an old brick building that housed the War Department. To the South, fronting 17th Street, was another old brick building occupied by the Navy Department. The space between the White House and the War Department building was a pleasant tree-lined park. The path from the White House to the War Department ran along the south end of this park, under a canopy formed by its many trees.

As a raw recruit with no previous military experience when he signed on with the Light Guard, Solomon had fully expected to be sent to an induction facility where he would receive basic military training. But instead, he and the other new members of the unit were sent directly to Washington. Although the unit's commissioned and non-commissioned officers were experienced military men and fully uniformed, Solomon and other new recruits were not issued uniforms until they reached their Washington barracks. One of the customers at his father's shop, a veteran who had served with the First Ohio Volunteer Infantry, had told Solomon of his own training when he enlisted in 1861. Solomon had expected to be assigned to the same facility, Camp Curtin, a Pennsylvania military installation where many Ohio recruits were trained. But in the current frenzied Civil War environment, most recruits were now being sent directly to their duty station. The few who were still sent to induction centers were usually there only long enough to be issued uniforms and assigned to a unit.

The week after his arrival in Washington, Solomon was summoned to the Treasury Building to cut the hair of Treasury Secretary Salmon P. Chase. A former governor of Ohio appointed to the treasury post by President Lincoln, Chase had closely monitored the mobilization of the Light Guard and was aware the unit travelled with its own barber.

After an initial visit that pleased him, Chase set up weekly appointments for shaves and haircuts. The secretary enjoyed chatting with his young fellow Ohioan, especially when he learned that Solomon was interested in business and finance. He frequently offered business advice, but when Solomon inquired about a job among the sea of clerks in the Treasury Department, Chase's attitude changed. He told Solomon that while he personally might be agreeable to having a Negro work as a clerk in the Treasury, he would have to further investigate to see if such an appointment could be made.

Over the next few weeks, Solomon had many opportunities to see Lincoln, and quite unexpectedly, would soon get to meet him. But from his first sighting, he was struck by the inadequacy of measures taken to protect the president. That first sighting came late one night during his second week in Washington. Standing guard near the front of the White House, Solomon saw the front door open. Dressed in a long, black frock coat and high silk hat, the president stepped out. He closed the door behind him and walked toward the front of the portico and stood alone in the darkness with his hands clasped behind his back. For several minutes he stood there, apparently in deep thought, unaware that anyone else might be nearby. He then took another few steps, stopping under a nearby gaslight.

Solomon could now see the president clearly. He looked weary. Although he was well over six feet in height, his long coat and high hat made him appear even taller. Beneath his hat, there bristled a mass of black hair, and his face was distinguished by a large nose, wide ears, and deeply set dark eyes. Despite a penetrating stare, his eyes seemed to project amiability and, perhaps, even gentleness.

The president came down the steps, and as he passed a nearby Light Guardsman, doffed his hat in recognition of the guard's salute. The guards appreciated how Lincoln, though not a military man, was always careful to return the salutes of soldiers. The president knew that his position as commander-in-chief entitled him to military honors. But he intuitively understood that the duty of a military leader to return a salute was as imperative as the duty of a soldier to give it.

The careworn president walked alone, as was his habit. He disappeared from view as he passed under the dense canopy of trees lining the park south of the White House. It was a long few moments before he reemerged from the shadows to enter the War Department building for his nightly war briefing. Because telegraph service had not yet been installed at the White House, the president found it necessary to go directly to the War Department to receive the most current wartime updates. Each morning and evening, he travelled the same route for his briefing, always coming and going in solitude.

During daylight hours, the walkway to the War Building was bright and cheery. Along the brick path there were sculptured shrubs and a view south, beyond President's Park of the majestic but still-unfinished Washington Monument. At night, however, the mood was completely different. Lit by a single gas jet, the route was ominous and unwelcoming. Reluctant to distrust his fellow Americans or suspect that any of them might attempt to harm him, it would not be until the spring of 1864 that Lincoln was finally convinced that he should be accompanied on these walks. Apparently, he was the last one to realize how easy it would have been for an assassin to kill him while he was on one of these solitary walks. Many months later, secessionist conspirators revealed that they were aware of the president's nighttime outings. They had planned to abduct him and hurry him across Treasury Park to a house belonging to a rebel sympathizer.

By the middle of November, Solomon had settled into a comfortable routine of Light Guard duty assignments and barbering for Secretary Chase and other unit members during his off hours. But all that changed abruptly the first week in January when the Corporal of the Guard ordered him to the White House with instructions to bring his barber tools. Solomon hurried from his guard post back to his barracks, gathered his tools, and reported to William Slade, the president's valet, confidential messenger, and confidant. The light-skinned Negro and long-time presidential aide had complete charge of the colored help and was responsible for making all arrangements for the president's public and private events. When Slade heard that a member of the Light Guard was a skilled barber, he immediately requested a meeting.

Slade carefully took the measure of Solomon. The distinguished White House staffer, an Elder at the prestigious 15th Street Presbyterian Church was impressed by Solomon's youthful good looks, olive complexion, and articulate conversation. "Thank you for taking the time to meet with me, young man," Slade began. "I know you are busy with your military responsibilities, but I understand you have barbering skills, and if that is true, it is a most fortuitous situation because the president has an urgent need for such services, and you may be just the man for the job."

"Yes, I am a trained barber," Solomon responded. "Not long ago, I completed my apprenticeship in the family shop.

"Excellent," responded the pompous aide with a lengthy clearing of his throat. "William Johnson, the man currently performing those duties will soon take on a new job. Although not trained as a barber, William has shaved the president and cut his hair for many years. But to many of us, the results are not always satisfactory, and Mr. Lincoln's hair and whiskers often look unkempt. We hope that, in the near future, you will be able to better serve the president."

What Slade failed to mention, and Solomon would later piece together from the president's own comments, is that Slade's dissatisfaction with William's services was more related to his dark skin than his barbering skills.

When he came to the White House as a newly elected president in 1861, Lincoln brought William with him. He was surprised and disappointed that William was not accepted by the White House's light-skinned Negro domestic staff. Grappling with his own evolving attitudes on the humanity and rights of Negroes, Lincoln was unprepared for the sometimes-uncharitable attitudes of the colored workers toward each other. He did not yet understand the persistent skin color prejudices among many black people that stemmed from privileged positions enjoyed by light-skinned, mixed-race children born to enslaved women who had been impregnated by their white masters. Unwilling to rock the boat of servant color hierarchy, Lincoln bowed to the concerns of his staff and found William a temporary position as a fireman in the White House furnace room. But with strong loyalty to his longtime aide, he wrote a governmental to-whom-it-may-concern letter soliciting a position for William, attesting to his honesty, integrity, faithfulness, and sobriety. When he received no responses, Lincoln spoke to several of his cabinet secretaries. Treasury Secretary Salmon Chase responded and had William hired as a laborer. Lincoln maintained contact with William, occasionally inviting him back to the White House when his regular valet had time off. On those occasions, Lincoln would pay William out of his own pocket.

With William seldom available, Slade suggested to the president that since the Light Guard barber was already working on the White House grounds as a guard and would be travelling with the president and his staff, he might make a good replacement barber. When the president concurred, Slade summoned Solomon. He immediately set up an appointment for the following day so that the president could meet Solomon and test his barbering skills.

Solomon arrived at the appointed time the next morning and was escorted by Slade to a second-floor corner office where President Lincoln sat, reading memos and letters at a cluttered desk. It was only 8:00 a.m., but the president looked as though he had been at work for several hours. He rose, smiled, and, in a courtly manner, extended his hand as Slade introduced Solomon.

"It's nice to meet you, Solomon," the president began. "I appreciate your willingness to attend to me on such short notice."

"The pleasure is all mine, Mr. President," Solomon quickly replied, trying his best to mirror Lincoln's easy smile and affability. "I'm happy to be able to serve you."

"How is it that you happen to be with the Light Guard and not with one of the colored units?" the president asked as he took his seat and gestured Slade and Solomon to a small nearby settee.

"I was recruited by the one of the colored Massachusetts volunteer regiments," Solomon responded, "but didn't pass the physical. When the Light Guard was assembled in my hometown of Columbus, one of its senior officers was familiar with my barbering and thought my skills would be useful in the new unit. He brought me in as part of quarter-master services."

"Yes, I heard about that from the same young captain," Lincoln responded. "He told me that you made a bit of a name for yourself in Columbus by breaking up a Blackbird kidnapping ring."

Amazed that the busy president who carried the weight of war and the fate of a nation on his shoulders was attuned to such details, Solomon stared silently at Lincoln and nodded. With no response to his words of praise, the president pivoted to a new topic.

"Solomon, I must meet with several members of congress later today, and I'd like to look decent enough to make my case. I see you have brought your tools with you. If you have the time, perhaps you can do something with my unruly hair and whiskers. I'm seriously challenged in matters of appearance, and I need all the help I can get," Lincoln added, lightening the moment with what Solomon would come to appreciate as the president's trademark self-deprecating wit.

"Of course," Solomon replied. "If you will kindly remove your tie and waistcoat, I'll move your chair closer to the window so I can work under natural light."

After sliding the president's heavy desk chair to a window that overlooked President's Park, Solomon laid out his tools. He took stock of the lanky president who appeared strongly built, but had stooping shoulders, long arms, large hands, and very large feet. As usual, the busy leader was dressed in a poorly fitting, wrinkled black suit that looked like an undertaker's uniform. His deeply furrowed brow, bristling chin whiskers, and wide protruding ears somehow projected an image of wisdom and kindliness. But the busy leader appeared neglected. Although he had a first lady and a valet to look after him, it did not appear to Solomon that the president had recently been the focus of anyone's tender loving care.

Solomon worked quickly and quietly over the next forty-five minutes. But the president seemed in no hurry, appearing to enjoy both the personal care and a few moments of tranquility in his otherwise busy and hectic day. When he inspected himself with a small mirror Solomon handed him, he liked what he saw. His beard was now evenly trimmed, the rest of his face clean-shaven, and his shortened hair neatly combed. He thanked Solomon and arranged for their next appointment.

In the coming days Solomon split his time between presidential guard duties and tonsorial services that involved shaving and trimming the president's whiskers three times per week and cutting his hair twice each month. Although working two jobs was demanding, it became a practice that Solomon would continue throughout his working career. In those days, a black man's salary was usually low, even for prestigious governmental service. Many found it necessary to work two or more jobs if they wanted to live above the bare subsistence level, especially if they were supporting a family.

Midway through Solomon's first month barbering for the president, William Slade requested his attendance at a White House staff meeting. The invitation was not to the weekly White House employees meeting regularly attended by some twenty-five administrative assistants and domestic workers, all of them white except for Slade and Elizabeth Keckley, the first lady's dressmaker. Instead, Solomon was to attend the colored help meeting which was held twice each month in an anteroom next to a basement kitchen. It included Slade, Cornella Mitchel, a cook, Peter Brown, a butler/waiter, Rosetta Wells, a seamstress, Solomon, and William Johnson.

Slade used his weekly meeting with colored workers to inform them of important issues discussed at the full staff meeting. At the first meeting attended by Solomon, the main topic was the White House stable fire that had occurred a week earlier, killing all the horses, ponies, and goats kept in the structure.

Lincoln had been one of the first to notice the fire, which had started around 8:30 p.m. Slade told the group how the president had sprung into action as soon as he spotted the blaze, running from the White House to the nearby stable and breaking open one of the doors with his bare hands. The fire department arrived at almost the same time, but none of the animals could be saved. Suspecting that the fire might have been set for the purpose of drawing Lincoln out of the White House to provide an opportunity to assassinate him, Solomon and a few of the other presidential guards on duty that night rushed the president back into the White House.

Slade informed the group that a coachman who had been fired by the president's wife earlier on the day of the fire, had been arrested on suspicion of arson. He also told of the president's despondency following the incident, as the favorite pony of his deceased twelve-year-old son, Willie, had died in the blaze. Lincoln still hadn't fully recovered from the melancholy in which he had been mired since Willie's passing. As Slade described the president's predicament, William Johnson teared up, trying as best he could to muffle his distress. When the others noticed William's tears, they berated him for his "false emotions."

Solomon was dumbfounded at their reaction. Throughout his short time in the White House, he had observed uncharitable, mean-spirited attitudes toward William exhibited by several of the other colored staff. William now had a new job as a laborer in the Treasury Department but occasionally attended Slade's meetings as, from time to time, he still served as one of the president's bodyguards and was called back to the White House when Lincoln's new valet had time off. As the newest person under Slade's supervision, Solomon had avoided speaking out in support of the somewhat docile William who was an able bodyguard and valet but unsuited for White House staff infighting. In the unpleasant moments of his first staff meeting, Solomon quickly recognized the motivation behind the disrespect directed at William.

Even though they held mostly menial jobs, the black White House staffers considered themselves the cream of Washington DC colored society. They were recognized as leaders in many churches, and fraternal and social organizations. Most were members of the 15th Street Presbyterian Church. All were light-complexioned, long-term employees who kept their positions as presidents came and went. They were a clannish group, so protective of their jobs when a new president took office that they resented all new employees, especially those who might be dark-skinned like William. It did not surprise Solomon that this group considered their light skin a point of pride that set them above their darker-skinned brethren. Clearly, they believed the more their skin color and facial features matched that of the dominant white class that ruled their world, the higher would be their social status and the faster would be their economic and political advancement.

Whether or not they approved of it, Solomon and many ambitious strivers like him recognized this as a dynamic within which they must live their lives and govern their behavior. Despite his recognition and acceptance of this harsh reality, Solomon wondered why the colored staff couldn't at least show William some compassion. They knew he had been the president's valet and companion throughout his son Willie's short and tragic life. Wasn't it understandable to them that he might still be feeling some of the pain suffered by his friend?

It was hard for Solomon to understand how these people could be so lacking in self-awareness that they felt no shame, whatsoever, for their false sense of superiority. They must have known that their light skin color was based solely on the many times that slave masters had violated their ancestors.

William never attended another meeting. Because his main duties were now at Treasury, the president wanted him to suffer no further staff abuse. Solomon continued to attend and never rebuked the group for its harsh treatment of William. As he was by far the youngest and the newest member of the group, Solomon didn't want to alienate the president or William Slade by becoming known around the White House as a hothead or a troublemaker.

Although he was usually protected by presidential guards when in the White House or visiting troops on the battlefield, at times the president would go out for carriage rides to visit the District of Columbia Old-Soldiers' Home, accompanied only by a driver. And through most of the war, he continued to worry the White House Light Guard contingent with his solitary, nightly walks to the War Department Building to get the latest battlefield updates.

Late in November of 1863, at the height of the war, just over four months after Union troops defeated Confederate forces at Gettysburg, Pennsylvania, Lincoln delivered a speech at the dedication of the Soldier's National Cemetery. The stirring address spanned only two-hundred-seventy-two words, the first six of which, "Four score and seven years ago," referred to the signing of the Declaration of Independence eighty-seven years earlier. The president's brief remarks portrayed the Civil War as a test of whether a nation dedicated to the proposition that all men were created equal could succeed. Lincoln considered the event and the opportunity to speak at the dedication a high point in his presidency.

The hopeful words of the short but impactful *Gettysburg Address* spread quickly throughout the US. To those opposed to slavery, the optimistic comments seemed to signal an early inflection point and possibly the beginning of the healing of a deeply divided nation. Many segments of a troubled public could hardly believe that a nation founded less than a century earlier to escape the tyranny of a foreign monarchy could now find itself at war with itself, Americans killing other Americans. Wasn't America intended to be a haven safe from oppression and inequality, they wondered? Perhaps Lincoln's positive and optimistic remarks foretold the end of the Civil War and the beginning of an extended period of heightened public consciousness in which inequality and racial oppression could never again exist. Solomon and others like him could only hope for such an outcome.

The very next week, William Johnson died. He had accompanied the President to Gettysburg, and during the visit, both he and Lincoln contracted Varioloid, a form of smallpox. Lincoln survived the illness, but William did not. Following his recovery, the president was clearly moved and in grief when Solomon next visited him for a shave and trim. Lincoln had always been troubled that the white House staff had never accepted William, his longest-serving aide. He asked Solomon why there was this kind of prejudice within Negro ranks. Solomon could offer no response other than to say he often puzzled over the same question. He was too embarrassed to acknowledge that the victims of racial oppression in America had adopted many of the prejudices of their oppressors.

III

Mrs. Keckley

When I was quite a child, an incident occurred that my mother afterward impressed more strongly on my mind. One of my uncles, a slave of Colonel Burwell, lost a pair of ploughlines, and when the loss was made known, the master gave him a new pair and told him that if he did not take care of them, he would punish him severely. In a few weeks the second pair of lines was stolen, and my uncle hung himself rather than meet the displeasure of his master. My mother went to the spring in the morning for a pail of water, and on looking up into the willow tree that shaded the bubbling stream, she discovered the lifeless body of her brother suspended beneath one of the strong branches. Rather than be punished the way Colonel Burwell punished his servants, he took his own life.

Elizabeth Keckley

As Solomon acclimated himself to the White House, he came to learn that not all the colored White House workers held the view that their fair complexion gave them privileged status. One such exception was Elizabeth Keckley, the first lady's personal dressmaker. While Mrs. Keckley was as light skinned if not lighter than most of the colored staff, her demeanor suggested that she believed her light complexion neither elevated nor diminished her status in the White House. The always elegantly attired and well-groomed modiste appeared completely comfortable in her skin. In their frequent chats in the succeeding months, Keckley shared her history and backstory with Solomon. Solomon appreciated her candor and support. She was only a few years younger than his own mother and was generous in providing tips on White House staff politics.

Solomon particularly appreciated how, through hard work and exceptional skill, Mrs. Keckley had elevated herself to the top levels of her trade. With no pedigree and no one opening doors for her, she worked her way into a White House position that most dressmakers could only dream of. Solomon understood and appreciated her journey, as he too had to work hard to excel in his trade and earn a position with the Light Guard. But while it was a happenchance military assignment that enabled him to become the president's barber, it was not a lucky break that allowed Mrs. Keckley to become the first lady's seamstress. Against great odds, she had fought and clawed her way to her goal. To Solomon, she was an inspirational figure.

Keckley was born into slavery in 1818 as Elizabeth Hobbs in a small Virginia town called Dinwiddie Court House. An only child, she and her mother, Agnes, were light-skinned house-slaves whose ancestors were kidnapped Africans and Southern white aristocrats. Their pigmentation marked them not only as slave property, but also as the product of generations of slave-breeding. Through serial rape of enslaved women, white masters had personally propagated and added to their slave stock while reinforcing their domination over both the victims of their disdainful lust and the men who had to live with the continuing abuse of their wives, mothers, and daughters.

In comparison to what most field slaves experienced—long, hard days under watchful eyes and cruel lashes of demanding overseers—Elizabeth enjoyed a relatively privileged childhood. She took care of her master's children, cleaned, cooked, laundered, and sewed. Exceptionally intelligent and attractive, Elizabeth developed an early interest in clothes. To the extent possible for a slave, she dressed well and enjoyed socializing. Having learned to read and write at a young age, her early letters often included descriptions of garments she had recently worn and new items she hoped to make for herself.

Elizabeth's mother, Agnes, was married to George Hobbs, an enslaved man who lived and worked on a nearby farm. Of course, Agnes and George were not legally married. By law, the enslaved were chattel, defined for congressional representation purposes as three-fifths human. For this reason, they couldn't enter into any legal contract, including marriage. However, Agnes's and George's owners recognized their relationship and allowed George to visit his wife twice a year. When his owner moved, George was separated from Agnes and Elizabeth. George and Agnes corresponded for many years, as both were literate. But, in time, his letters stopped coming, and the family never saw or heard from him again. Elizabeth mourned George's absence and treasured his letters. Years later she wrote:

> The most precious mementos of my existence are the faded old letters he wrote, full of love and always hoping that the future would bring brighter days.

Agnes was a talented seamstress who made clothes for the family of her owner, Armistead Burwell, and the seventy slaves he owned. Before her death, Agnes revealed that Burwell was Elizabeth's father.

At age fourteen, Elizabeth was loaned to Burwell's eldest son, Robert, her white half-brother. Robert's wife, Anne, resented how closely Elizabeth resembled Robert. Irked by what she perceived as Elizabeth's overly strong-willed demeanor, Anne called in a neighbor to "break" the young slave. But Elizabeth did not docilely accept beatings. Guided by her instinct that the master preferred whipping those who were most easily whipped, she refused to strip down to receive her punishment and struggled with her abuser until he overpowered, tied, and bound her.

Although she was beaten repeatedly, Elizabeth never begged for mercy or even acknowledged pain. Finally, during one particularly vicious beating, her exhausted punisher broke into tears, apologized for his cruelty, and promised to never strike her again. To Elizabeth, the tearful confession was less a sincere apology than an expression of frustration and humiliation over his failure to break her. Even though she bore the bruises of the beating, in an odd way, she had turned the tables and broken her abuser. He probably would never have apologized had she bent to his will.

At eighteen, Elizabeth was sent to work for Alexander Kirkland, a friend of her owner to whom she was forced to become a concubine. Out of that liaison came a son who Elizabeth named George, after her stepfather. The product of the rape of many generations of his enslaved ancestors, young George's racial identity was hopelessly blurred. After attending Wilberforce University, he would use his father's name and join the Union Army as a white man. He would be killed in the Battle of Wilson's Creek in Missouri on August 10, 1861, shortly after he enlisted.

Kirkland died when his son was eighteen months old. Elizabeth and her slave child were then sent to serve Armistead Burwell's daughter, Anne, (Elizabeth's half-sister) and her attorney husband, Hugh Garland. Elizabeth's new duties reunited her with her mother, but when Garland fell on hard times and moved the family to St. Louis, he threatened to rent Agnes out. Faced with the prospect of once again being separated from Agnes, Elizabeth wrote:

My mother, my poor aged mother, go among strangers to toil for a living! No, a thousand times no! I would rather work my fingers to the bone, bend over my sewing till the film of blindness gathered in my eyes; nay even beg from street to street. I told Mr. Garland so, and he gave me permission to see what I could do.

What Elizabeth did was to become a successful modiste. Taught and spurred on by her mother, the ambitious young woman became an accomplished seamstress. Working long hours every day after her household duties, she began a dressmaking career by sewing and designing clothes for white women in the St. Louis area. In time, she accumulated a loyal group of customers and was not only able to prevent her mother from being hired out, but also to keep food on the table for Garland's family of seventeen.

After more than two years of caring for his family, usually as the primary subsistence provider, Elizabeth asked Garland to allow her to purchase her freedom. The struggling lawyer was not anxious to cooperate, but knew that one way or another, he would soon lose his meal ticket. He offered Elizabeth a quarter to pay for the ferry trip that would take her across the Mississippi River to Illinois where slavery was illegal, a dismissive gesture intended to show her that, despite his dire financial straits, her freedom could only be achieved by his generosity. But there were other reasons for his offer.

Fleeing to Illinois would put Elizabeth in violation of the Fugitive Slave Act. A provision of this act allowed any slaveholder or his agent, or anyone posing as such, to claim any Negro as a fugitive slave by presenting an affidavit of ownership that a justice of the peace recognized as valid. Slaves recovered in this manner were subjected to punishment and severe restrictions. Because officers of the court were paid ten dollars by the federal government for each slaveholder claim they accepted, and only five dollars for each rejection, they had great incentive to return all slaves to their owners, even those whose ownership might be in doubt.

Mitigating even further against leaving the Garlands as a fugitive was the recently decided Dred Scott Case. Dred Scott and his wife, both enslaved, had been taken by their owner from Missouri into the Missouri Territory, a "free territory." When they were later brought back to Missouri, Scott sued in court in 1852, claiming that because he and his wife had been taken into free territory, he had been automatically freed and was no longer a slave. After two lower courts rejected his suit, he sued in the U.S. Supreme Court, which ruled against him in the infamous *Dred Scott Decision of 1857*. The decision stated that Negroes:

> ... had for more than a century before been regarded as beings of an inferior order, and altogether unfit to associate with the white race, either in social or political relations; and so far inferior, that they had no rights which the white man was bound to respect; and that the negro might justly and lawfully be reduced to slavery for his benefit. He was bought and sold, and treated as an ordinary article of merchandise and traffic, whenever a profit could be made by it.

The decision further claimed that Negroes:

> ...are not included, and were not intended to be included, under the word 'citizens' in the Constitution, and can therefore claim none of the rights and privileges which that instrument provides for and secures to citizens of the United States.

Ironically, Hugh Garland was the attorney for the defendant, and it was he who won the decision by which the Scott petition was denied. Elizabeth knew that, as a fugitive, she would have to depend on Garland's continued favor and cooperation to remain free. She did not want to take that chance and continued to press him to allow her to purchase her freedom. Finally, in 1852, Garland agreed to free Elizabeth for a price of $1,200. She raised the funds from savings and customer loans. Her insistence on buying her freedom stood in stark contrast to the position of other prominent formerly enslaved, like Frederick Douglass who argued strongly against paying even one cent for the freedom entitled to them by God's law, the Declaration of Independence, and the United States Constitution. Upon securing the agreement for her freedom, Elizabeth married John Keckley, a man she believed to be a free-born Negro.

On August 13, 1855, Elizabeth's "free papers" were drawn up and the transaction executed.

> Know ye all men that I, Anne P. Garland of the County and City of St. Louis, State of Missouri, for and in consideration of the sum of $1200, to me in hand paid this day in cash, hereby emancipate my Negro woman Lizzie and her son George.
>
> The said Lizzie is known in St. Louis as the wife of James, who is called James Keckley, is of light complexion, about 37 years of age, by trade a dress-maker and called by those who know her Garland's Lizzie. The said boy, George is the only child of Lizzie, is almost white and called by those who know him Garland's George.
>
> Witness my hand and seal, this 15th day of November, 1855
> Anne P. Garland
>
> Witness: John Wickham

Unfortunately, Elizabeth and her husband were never a good fit. The hard-working, almost driven Elizabeth was worlds apart from John, an alcoholic who lived what Elizabeth deemed a dissipated life. Although he had represented himself to her as a freedman, she later found out he was a fugitive slave, a life she had rejected for herself when she insisted upon purchasing her freedom from Hugh Garland instead of escaping to St. Louis. After eight years of marriage, the Keckleys went their separate ways.

Elizabeth became an active member of the colored community and devoted herself not only to her business but also to community service. She joined the First African Baptist Church which ran a secret school for Negroes. Under the cover of a sewing class, she taught reading and writing. But she was not happy. She had split with her husband, and her son, George, had gone off on his own. Worse yet, Hugh Garland had died, and his widow had taken Elizabeth's mother to Mississippi.

Elizabeth gave up her thriving business and travelled more than eight hundred miles to Baltimore where she tried to start a sewing school to teach her system of dress design and construction. But a few months later, she gave up on her plans and moved to Washington, DC. Among the wives, daughters, and mistresses of the political elite, she found many new clients eager to purchase her fashionable and original designs. She performed services for women of all political stripes, from Varina Davis, wife of Confederate leader Jefferson Davis, to Hannah Sumner, wife of Union General Edwin Sumner. To the socially active and prideful Elizabeth, pedigree and ability to pay was more important than politics. When Mrs. Davis invited her to relocate to the South where her husband was soon to become the president of the Confederacy, Elizabeth demurred. She preferred to cast her lot with the people of the North, and she soon became Mary Todd Lincoln's personal seamstress, friend, and advisor.

Elizabeth became an integral part of Washington DC Negro leadership, enjoying friendships with prominent leaders such as Frederick Douglass and Henry Highland Garnet. Known in DC business and social circles as Madame Keckley, she helped cement her business credentials by positioning her dressmaking establishment next door to that of a Madame Estern, a prestigious "colored fashionable hairdresser." Because of their access to the wealthy and powerful, nineteenth century barbers, beauticians, and dressmakers of color enjoyed social status equal to teachers and lawyers.

Elizabeth was more than just an ambitious striver who used her business to enhance her social status and her social status to leverage more business. She had become a member of what W. E. B. DuBois would later describe as *The Talented Tenth*, the one in ten Negroes who would lead the race. Elizabeth established her leadership credentials and her commitment to community service with the founding of the *Contraband Relief Association.*

Because of her own history, Elizabeth had long sympathized with former slaves, or "contraband," as they were called, who fled to Washington during the Civil War. Her association gathered funds and clothing for poor ex-slaves. Her motivation for creating her relief association is described in her own words in a passage from the autographical *Behind the Scenes, or Thirty Years a Slave, and Four Years in the White House,* a book she wrote while in Mrs. Lincoln's service and later published in 1868.

> One fair summer evening I was walking the streets of Washington, accompanied by a friend, when a band of music was heard in the distance. We wondered what it could mean, and curiosity prompted us to find out its meaning. We quickened our steps and discovered that it came from the house of Mrs. Farnham. The yard was brilliantly lighted, ladies and gentlemen were moving about, and the band was playing some of its sweetest airs. We approached the sentinel on duty at the gate, and asked what was going on. He told us that it was a festival given for the benefit of the sick and wounded soldiers in the city. This suggested an idea to me. If the white people can give festivals to raise funds for the relief of suffering soldiers, why should not the well-to-do colored people go to work to do something for the benefit of the suffering blacks? I could not rest. The thought was ever present with me, and the next Sunday I made a suggestion in the colored church, that a society of colored people be formed to labor for the benefit of the unfortunate freedmen. The idea proved popular, and in

two weeks "the Contraband Relief Association" was organized, with forty working members.

———————

Friendship with Elizabeth Keckley had great impact on Solomon. In the years prior to coming to the White House, he had known many ex-slaves. Some had been freed by their masters, some had bought their release, and some were runaways. Many were the product of slave rape. His conversations with them had always centered on the evils of slavery and the ongoing struggle for freedom but never broached the awkward topic of perceived skin color advantages associated with racial mixing. With Mrs. Keckley's lived experience, maturity, and balanced sense of self-awareness, Solomon had finally found someone who might be able to discuss and shed light on the delicate topic.

When the two got a chance to discuss the matter, Mrs. Keckley began by referencing the sad notion of black self-deprecation popularized by the old wives' tale of the Negroes who travelled across town to purchase ice from a white iceman instead of buying from a colored vendor in their own neighborhood. When asked their reason for shunning the local iceman, they claimed "The white man's ice is colder."

"Even though most colored people laugh at that anecdote, truly believing that only the most ignorant handkerchief-head could actually think such nonsense, there are many who buy into white superiority, often unconsciously but sometimes intentionally," Mrs. Keckley explained to Solomon. "Most colored folks will never admit it, but after generations of being beaten down, disrespected, and treated as property, many have come to not question the white man's top dog status. Sadly, many who have been emancipated still live under such a spell.

"Many under that 'spell' act out their self-loathing by trying to emulate the white man," Keckley continued. "Often that emulation shows in a Negro's pride in having skin color close to that of the master; the closer the better. Worst of all is when those who are closest in color to the white man look down on those who are darker. It is tragic for anyone to think this way, since in most cases, light skin results from the slave-rape of one's ancestors. I don't have to tell you that there is much of this skin-color superiority foolishness going on with the same White House colored staff that shunned and mistreated William Johnson so badly. On several occasions, I've had to call some of them to account for their behavior. To avoid embarrassing them in front of white staff, I try to discuss such matters in private, especially since they work for Mr. Slade, not me."

Solomon thanked Mrs. Keckley for her frank opinions on a matter they would continue to discuss from time to time. He told her how much he appreciated her outspokenness and her attempts to sensitize colored staff on such a delicate matter. He told her that, at times, he worried that her frank talk about racial issues might get her into trouble. He admitted that even though he fully shared her views, he would be reluctant to express them in the White House.

"I've got a bit more leeway to be outspoken than most because the person I work for, the first lady, is nothing if not outspoken," Mrs. Keckley responded. "You, however, have a different situation. The president is a shrewd, brilliant leader who is determined to end slavery. But he's still a white man who doesn't currently, and may never in the future, see the Negro as his equal. Around him, you will have to be more cautious with your words."

IV

The Black Republican

If I could save the Union without freeing any slave I would do it; and if I could save it by freeing all the slaves I would do it; and if I could save it by freeing some of the slaves and leaving others alone I would also do that. What I do about slavery, and the colored race, I do because I believe it helps to save the Union.

Abraham Lincoln – 1862

I am naturally anti-slavery. If slavery is not wrong, nothing is wrong. I can not remember when I did not so think and feel.

Abraham Lincoln – 1864

While Lincoln enjoyed the haircuts and shaves that gave him a few moments of quiet respite from the cares of his office, there were occasions when he would meet with cabinet members or receive briefings while Solomon was performing his work. At times, the serenity of the president's care was interrupted by the sudden appearance of the first lady, who frequently embarrassed her husband with outbursts over trivial matters that were usually none of her concern. In Solomon's presence, she sometimes even scolded the president about his speeches and public remarks and once berated him for conversation he had shared with a woman he encountered at a social event.

Solomon wished he could disappear when Mrs. Lincoln attacked her husband in this way. The first lady had been in a bad state ever since her son Willie's passing, a situation that had worsened the depression she had fallen into after the previous death of another son, Eddie, twelve years earlier. Solomon could only imagine the pain also felt by the president who had not only suffered the same losses, but now had to withstand his wife's abuse while prosecuting a war and laboring to keep the country together.

Over the course of the following months, as the war raged on, Solomon came to appreciate the president's calm leadership of a nation in conflict. Although Lincoln had received less than one year of formal schooling and had no training or experience in conducting a war, by the power of his own intellect and will, he had become an excellent strategist and wartime leader.

As he quietly performed his duties, Solomon witnessed many frank discussions involving Lincoln and his senior staff. These discussions helped him understand and appreciate the president's unusual talents. During the early days of the war, there had been great concern that Lincoln was no match for his rebel counterpart, Confederate President Jefferson Davis, who was a West Point graduate and a former Secretary of War. Davis's initial presidential advantage was punctuated by his early selection of General Robert E. Lee to lead the Confederate Army. The Union forces were initially led by General George McClellan who had been hurriedly pressed into a leadership role after an unexpected Confederate victory in the Civil War's first major confrontation, the Battle of Bull Run, fought only thirty miles south of Washington, DC.

McClellan proved to be not only ineffective on the battlefield, but socially and politically inept. He and Lincoln shared a mutual distrust and disdain for each other. The ambitious general's many strategic military blunders included a squandered opportunity to destroy Lee's Confederate forces at the 1862 Battle of Antietam. In the crucial early engagement, McClellan refused to attack and instead wanted to negotiate for peace. He told his staff: "I can work this out. Lincoln doesn't understand these things the way I do."

Shocked and angry at the insubordination, Lincoln confronted McClellan. "Why did you not pursue Lee? You could have destroyed him on the battlefield, but now the war could go on for years."

The president never received a good response but addressed his leadership problem by quickly forming his own big-picture assessment of the war, an independent evaluation that proved uncannily accurate. He moved, without hesitation, to take full advantage of the Union's advantages over the South, its greater number of troops, its more abundant natural resources, and its superior sea power. He immediately mobilized 400,000 troops and imposed a naval blockade of the Confederacy. Two years into the war, he tightened the screws on the Confederacy when he appointed Ulysses Grant as Union Army Commanding General. With that change, Lincoln finally had the battlefield leader he wanted. At that point, his confidence increased that the South would eventually go down in defeat.

As a Light Guardsman, Solomon particularly appreciated the president's devotion to Union soldiers. In addition to the way he returned the salutes of all soldiers with a bow or touch of his hat, he treated men in uniform as equals and always exhibited concern for their welfare. Known for a heavy travel schedule that often involved the delivery of important addresses, Lincoln had recently journeyed to Maryland to issue the Emancipation Proclamation, which freed slaves in Confederate States, and to Pennsylvania for his Gettysburg Address. He also frequently took more dangerous trips to Civil War battlefields where he met with his generals and visited wounded soldiers, both Union and Confederate. On those trips he could usually hear the sounds of cannon fire and occasionally would come under fire himself.

On one such trip to Fort Stevens in Washington DC, Lincoln was standing on one of the fort's parapets, an army doctor next to him, when Confederates began their assault. In the ensuing firefight, a Confederate sharpshooter wounded the doctor with a shot through the thigh. As enemy fire continued and Lincoln remained in place, ordering troops to fall back, a young Captain Oliver Wendell Holmes, perhaps not recognizing who he was addressing, shouted at the president: "Get down, you damn fool!" After the battle, as the president left the fort, he said good-bye to the future Supreme Court Justice, adding: "I'm glad to see you know how to talk to a civilian."

What Solomon most appreciated was how the service of colored troops seemed to affect Lincoln's evolving racial outlook. Lincoln got his first look at black soldiers in the field when he visited Union Army Headquarters in City Point, Virginia. He later observed:

> I was opposed on nearly every side when I first favored the raising of colored regiments, but they have proved their efficiency, and I am glad they have kept pace with the white troops in recent assaults. When we wanted every able-bodied man who could be spared to go to the front, and my opposers kept objecting to the Negroes, I told them at such times it was just as well to be color-blind.

Although Lincoln had earlier been a supporter of the Fugitive Slave Act of 1850, he now demanded of his generals that colored soldiers be treated the same as white soldiers, even though that equal treatment would not extend to equal pay until black troops threatened mutiny. When the Confederacy declared that Negroes bearing arms would be treated as insurrectionary slaves and likely executed, Lincoln issued a *Re-*

taliatory Order stipulating that "for every soldier of the United States killed in violation of the laws of war, a rebel soldier shall be executed." In his continuing evolution, he suspended prisoner of war exchanges when the Confederates sought to limit exchanges to whites.

Black soldiers valued the president's faith in them. On one occasion when his carriage passed a brigade of Negro troops, they shouted, in a spontaneous outburst of affection: "Hurrah for the liberator! Hurrah for the President!" Lincoln was touched, his eyes brimming with tears and his voice cracking as he talked with the men. To him, the presence of colored soldiers served as testament to the Emancipation Proclamation. In a speech to a crowd in his Springfield, Illinois hometown, he addressed critics of emancipation:

> You say you will not fight to free Negroes. Well, some of them seem willing to fight for you.... I thought that in your struggle for the Union, to whatever extent the Negroes should cease helping the enemy, to that extent it weakened the enemy in his resistance to you. Do you think differently? I thought that whatever Negroes can be got to do as soldiers, leaves just so much less for white soldiers to do, in saving the Union. Does it appear otherwise to you? But Negroes, like other people, act upon motives. Why should they do anything for us if we will do nothing for them? If they stake their lives for us, they must be prompted by the strongest motive: the promise of freedom. And the promise being made, must be kept.

Solomon was not surprised that Lincoln was smart and instinctively shrewd. It seemed clear that without such strengths, it would have been impossible for an unsophisticated Illinois woodsman like him to have ascended to the presidency. What Solomon had not expected was Lincoln's down-to-earth humility and humanity. Unlike the self-important members of his cabinet, an ambitious and competitive group jealous of him and other, Lincoln's unpretentious and empathetic demeanor made him likeable to the leadership class and common folk alike. With his characteristic humor and wit, he was able to parry and even redirect the scorn and ridicule of critics to his own advantage.

But not everyone appreciated the president's humor. In the early years of the Civil War, a congressman had called on Lincoln to air his concerns about a particular Union Army setback. When the president began his response by relating an anecdote, the congressman, James Ashley, interrupted. "Mr. President, I did not come here this morning to hear stories. It is too serious a time."

The president quickly fired back: "Ashley, sit down! I respect you as an earnest, sincere man. You cannot be more anxious than I have been constantly since the beginning of the war; and I say to you now, that were it not for this occasional release, I should die."

Sometimes the pushback came from the cabinet, Secretary of State Willis Seward, Secretary of the Treasury Salmon Chase, and Secretary of War Simeon Cameron, each of whom had sought the presidency and harbored serious reservations about Lincoln's limited administrative and military qualifications. When Chase visited him at the White House to discuss concerns about war expenditures on the Treasury, the president suggested that the solution might be to: "give your paper mill another turn." The lighthearted suggestion that the problem might be solved simply by printing more money upset the self-righteous Chase.

Aware that Chase was positioning himself to succeed him in the 1864 election, Lincoln ignored the secretary's repeated petty and disrespectful comments. To his personal secretary, he commented about the negative remarks: "I have determined to shut my eyes, so far as possible, to everything of the sort. Mr. Chase makes a good Treasury Secretary, and I shall keep him where he is. If he becomes president, all right. I hope we will never have a worse man." In time, Lincoln's steadfastness, iron will, humility, and his ability to rise to the expectations of the moment caused many of his detractors to acknowledge his exceptionalism.

Secretary of State Seward would later describe Lincoln as "the best man of us all."

Solomon had often heard Lincoln called "The Northern Railsplitter," a derisive reference to his early work felling and splitting trees to make fence rails. The name was intended to depict Lincoln as a country bumpkin unfit to hold high office. But Lincoln embraced the name, often campaigning with it to promote his image as a leader who understood and appreciated the challenges faced by the working man. At times he made gifts of the rough metal wedges used by woodsmen to split rails. He even had one inscribed with the initials: *AL.*

In time, Lincoln earned a few additional titles. Many referred to him as *Lincoln Africanus* because of his evolving attitudes on slavery and emancipation, and *King Abraham* for using executive action to work around an uncooperative congress. In an attempt to tie black liberation to the Republicans, political foes labelled him *The Black Republican.*

Solomon particularly enjoyed Lincoln's deflection of the Black Republican reference. The characterization had first been used against him by Steven Douglas in 1858 when the two battled for an Illinois seat in the US Senate, a race that Lincoln subsequently lost. In their famous debate series, Douglas criticized Lincoln and others who shared his views. The diminutive senator labeled them abolitionists, foes of a state's right to choose for itself whether or not it would allow slavery. Douglas's criticism was in response to Lincoln's *House Divided* speech in which the president claimed:

> A house divided against itself cannot stand. I believe this government cannot endure, permanently half slave and half free. I do not expect the Union to be dissolved—I do not expect the House to fall—but I do expect it will cease to be divided. It will become all one thing, or all the other.

But still troublingly conflicted in his racial attitudes, on another occasion he also said:

> I am not, nor ever have been in favor of making voters of the Negroes, or jurors, or qualifying them to hold office, or having them to marry with white people.

While Lincoln never wavered in his own racial identity, his evolving attitudes allowed him to embrace the Black Republican label. He had always identified as a staunch Republican, but at times he now also referred to himself as a "long black fellow" and sometimes even described his complexion as "dark."

———◦———

Although Solomon appreciated Lincoln's expanding attitudes on race, he recognized that the president was still a work in progress, often pursuing conflicting and incompatible objectives. In 1862, when the war had been going poorly for the Union, the president had issued the celebrated proclamation that freed slaves in all Confederate states and provided no compensation to their former owners. The proclamation dealt a major blow to the Confederacy, but also presented a serious problem to the president as he provided no plan as to what was to become of all the freed slaves.

Although Lincoln strongly opposed slavery, he did not believe that black and white races could integrate successfully. In his view, it would be impossible for white America to absorb nearly four million former slaves. To quiet the fears of white citizens that America would be "Africanized"—overrun by freed Negroes—Lincoln came up with a Negro colonization plan to deport the colored population to destinations outside the US. The concept had been earlier popularized by the American Colonization Society whose past members included former U.S. presidents Thomas Jefferson, James Madison, and James Monroe. The proposed program was investigated by a nine-member House of Representatives Select Committee on Emancipation and Colonization. The committee enthusiastically supported the concept, opining that there was little hope that the Negro could ever be accepted into the American way of life. As they put it, he would always be thought of as a slave, a notion kept alive "by the changeless color of the Ethiope's skin."

Even though, by now, most Americans of color had been born on US soil, Lincoln favored shipping them to Central America, the Caribbean, or Africa. In a Eulogy for the statesman Henry Clay, he said:

> If as the friends of colonization hope, we succeed in freeing our land from the presence of slavery; and, at the same time, in restoring a captive people to their long-lost fatherland, it will indeed be a glorious consummation.

A few months before he issued the Emancipation Proclamation, Lincoln called together a small group of Negro leaders to discuss the colonization plan and enlist their support. It was the first time that a US president had ever invited such a group to meet with him at the White House. Lincoln opened the meeting to the press to ensure that its outcomes would be publicized.

The five invitees were leading members of Washington's Negro community. Oddly, Frederick Douglass was not one of them. The president likely was unaware that three of the five invitees were Prince Hall Masons, members of black Masonic lodges recently formed in defiance of the traditional Masonic order that excluded Negroes, and in the South, still supported slavery. Two of the three: Delegation Leader Edward Thomas and John T. Costin had served as Grand Masters of Prince Hall Masons in the District, and the third, John F. Cook, would do so in the future. Because Prince Hall Masonic lodges opposed slavery and, on occasions, secretly functioned as Underground Railroad stops, many Negroes did not publicly acknowledge their Masonic involvement. In this way, they avoided Fugitive Slave Law violations.

After introductions, Lincoln spoke to the delegation of his deep opposition to slavery, which he believed to be in direct conflict with American ideals. He had expressed these long-standing views on many occasions prior to the meeting. Early in the civil war, he had said: "I am naturally anti-slavery. If slavery is not wrong, nothing is wrong. I cannot remember when I did not so think and feel." But he had also expressed his belief that emancipated slaves would be a "troublesome presence" in America.

The president informed the group that $600,000 had been appropriated by Congress and placed at his disposition "for the purpose of aiding the colonization in some country of the people, or a portion of them, of African descent, thereby making it his duty, as it had for a long time been his inclination, to favor that cause."

"You and we are different races," he told his colored guests. "Your race suffers very greatly ... while ours suffers from your presence. In a word, we suffer on both sides. It is better for us both to be separated."

Simultaneously astounding his guests and straining their credulity, Lincoln continued his odd rationalization: "But for your race among us there could not be war, although many men engaged on either side do not care for you one way or the other. Nevertheless, I repeat, without the institution of slavery and the colored race as a basis, the war could not have an existence."

His guests listening in stunned silence as the president continued with carefully prepared remarks that placed blame for the Civil War squarely on slaves, not their enslavers:

> It is better for us both, therefore, to be separated. I know that there are free men among you, who even if they could better their condition are not as much inclined to go out of the country as those, who being slaves could obtain their freedom on this condition. I suppose one of the principal difficulties in the way of colonization is that the free colored man cannot see that his comfort would be advanced by it. You may believe you can live in Washington or elsewhere in the United States the remainder of your life as easily, perhaps more so than you can in any foreign country, and hence you may come to the conclusion that you have noth-

ing to do with the idea of going to a foreign country. This is, I speak in no unkind sense, an extremely selfish view of the case.

But you ought to do something to help those who are not so fortunate as yourselves. There is an unwillingness on the part of our people, harsh as it may be, for you free colored people to remain with us. Now, if you could give a start to white people, you would open a wide door for many to be made free. If we deal with those who are not free at the beginning, and whose intellects are clouded by slavery, we have very poor materials to start with. If intelligent colored men, such as are before me, would move in this matter, much might be accomplished. It is exceedingly important that we have men at the beginning capable of thinking as white men, and not those who have been systematically oppressed....

Lincoln paused to let his guests fully absorb his message. He looked for some sign of acceptance or possibly even approval. But he got none. Recognizing that the cold stares directed at him were not a good sign, he soldiered on.

The place I am thinking about having for a colony is in Central America. It is nearer to us than Liberia—not much more than one-fourth as far as Liberia, and within seven days' run by steamers. Unlike Liberia it is on a great line of travel—it is a highway. The country is a very excellent one for any people, and with great natural resources and advantages, and especially because of the similarity of climate with your native land—thus being suited to your physical condition.

The particular place I have in view is to be a great highway from the Atlantic or Caribbean Sea to the Pacific Ocean, and this particular place has all the advantages for a colony. On both sides there are harbors among the finest in the world. Again, there is evidence of very rich coal mines. A certain amount of coal is valuable in any country, and there may be more than enough for the wants of the country. Why I attach so much importance to coal is, it will afford an opportunity to the inhabitants for immediate employment till they get ready to settle permanently in their homes....

I shall, if I get a sufficient number of you engaged, have provisions made that you shall not be wronged. If you will engage in the enterprise I will spend some of the money entrusted to me.

Any hope that the president might convince the delegation that Colonization would benefit Negroes ended when he expressed doubts about his own proposal.

I am not sure you will succeed. The government may lose the money, but we cannot succeed unless we try; but we think, with care, we can succeed.

The political affairs in Central America are not in quite as satisfactory a condition as I wish. There are contending factions in that quarter; but it is true all the factions are agreed alike on the subject of colonization, and want it, and are more generous than we are here. To your colored race they have no objection. Besides, I would endeavor to have you made equals, and have the best assurance that you should be the equals of the best.

The practical thing I want to ascertain is whether I can get a number of able-bodied men, with their wives and children, who are willing to go, when I present evidence of encouragement and protection. Could I get a hundred tolerably intelligent men, with their wives and children, to 'cut their own fodder,' so to speak? Can I have fifty? If I could find twenty-five able-bodied men, with a mixture of women and children, good things in the family relation, I think I could make a successful commencement.

I want you to let me know whether this can be done or not. This is the practical part of my wish to see you. These are subjects of very great importance, worthy of a month's study instead of a speech delivered in an hour. I ask you then to consider seriously not pertaining to yourselves merely, nor for your race, and ours, for the present time, but as one of the things, if successfully managed, for the good of mankind—not confined to the present generation.

At the end of Lincoln's presentation, the delegation sat in stone-faced silence and shock. His proposal, simultaneously demeaning and patronizing, was not well-received. The leader of the group, Edward Thomas, curtly replied that "they would hold a consultation and in a short time give an answer."

"Take your full time—no hurry at all" the president responded. The delegation then left with no further discussion.

Negroes did not react well to Lincoln's pronouncements. As soon as he heard about the meeting, Frederick Douglass wrote scornfully about the strategy in *Douglas Monthly*, one of four newspapers he published, all of them dedicated to abolitionism and social reform. Douglass labeled Lincoln's plan a trick by slaveholders.

In this address Mr. Lincoln assumes the language and arguments of an itinerant Colonization lecturer, showing all his inconsistencies, his pride of race and blood, his contempt for Negroes and his canting hypocrisy... though elected as an anti-slavery man by Republican and Abolition voters, Mr. Lincoln is quite a genuine representative of American prejudice and Negro hatred and far more concerned for the preservation of slavery, and the favor of the Border Slave States, than for any sentiment of magnanimity or principle of justice and humanity.

Responding explicitly to the assertion that the presence of the Negro in America was the cause of the Civil War, Douglass ridiculed Lincoln, stating:

> A horse thief pleading the existence of the horse as the apology for his theft, or a highwayman contending that the money in the traveler's pocket is the sole first cause of his robbery are about as much entitled to respect as is the President's reasoning at this point.

Douglass's biting and unrelenting presidential criticism was not restricted to his own publications but was widely printed in national and local newspapers ranging from the black-published Washington *Bee* to the conservative *Evening Star*. Solomon read this coverage with great interest, and as much as he continued to respect and support the president's principled and evolving national leadership on slavery and race, he could not deny the cogency of Douglass's compelling and well-reasoned attack. His interest sparked by Douglass's most recent explosive comments, Solomon became fascinated by the wide-ranging insights and wisdom of the fiery black leader. The more he read of Douglass's comments and recommendations, the more he hoped that the controversial black leader might come together with President Lincoln to pursue what, in many cases, were common objectives. He was encouraged to learn from William Slade that the two might soon meet.

Earlier State Department inquiries initiated by Lincoln among African and South American governments regarding colonization apparently had yielded positive responses only from Liberia, Panama, and *Ile a Vache*, ("Cow Island"), a small, 20-square-mile island off the southwestern coast of Haiti. Several other proposed recipient nations viewed

Lincoln's proposal as an affront, an attempt by the US to use them as a dumping ground for its own race problems.

Despite the many misgivings expressed by Douglass and other black leaders, the night before he issued the Emancipation Proclamation, Lincoln signed an agreement with a Florida cotton planter to relocate five thousand former slaves to Ile a Vache. Federal funds would be provided to cover the costs. A few months later, the *Ocean Ranger* departed from Fortress Monroe, Virginia. With 453 hopeful Negro emigrants aboard, they headed for Ile a Vache.

The mission was a complete and unmitigated failure. By the time the *Ocean Ranger* reached its destination, thirty passengers had died from smallpox. A second ship that was to have accompanied the *Ocean Ranger* carrying building and living supplies never set sail. Even worse, the self-appointed superintendent of the island had misled the government and the settlers about living conditions. Houses had been promised, but instead families had to sleep on the bare earth in bush huts. The superintendent paid wages in a bogus currency which workers could only spend on overpriced foods and supplies in a company store. When the workers threatened revolt, the superintendent fled the island.

Based on the failure of the Ile a Vache misadventure, further colonization efforts were put on hold. But the president never gave up on the idea. He continued to think about the initiative, and often sought advice on the project from trusted advisors.

Usually, Solomon performed his barbering duties quietly, listening intently but not involving himself in any of the discussions between the president and his visitors. But on one instance in late January of 1864, he was surprised to be pulled into a conversation in which he was neither eager nor prepared to participate. The occasion involved a visit by Secretary of State Seward to discuss the colonization of Negroes. Through Lincoln's conversation with Seward during an early morning haircut, Solomon had pieced together the president's long-range plan for Negroes in America.

It had been almost ten years since Lincoln had first floated his colonization proposal. Since he hadn't yet received even the slightest signal of interest from any black leader, as Solomon cut his hair at today's meeting with Secretary Seward, Lincoln discussed whether the idea of colonization should finally be put to rest. At a momentary lull in the conversation, the president glanced at Solomon and caught his eye. Sensing from his uncharacteristically slow barbering that Solomon was reacting to the conversation, Lincoln asked him, point-blank, for his opinion.

"Solomon, I don't want to put you on the spot, but I need your honest opinion. Wouldn't an ambitious young fellow like you be interested in escaping the wounds and ill-will of a nation scarred by slavery so that you could move on for a fresh start in a new land of opportunity?"

The request was completely unexpected. In the few weeks Solomon had worked for the president, he had shared no more conversation than cordial greetings and responses to direct questions about his services. Still only nineteen, he felt unbelievably lucky just to be standing in the president's office and witnessing so many important discussions. Now he was being asked for his opinion on a delicate political concept that he personally found reprehensible, but that the president favored and sought to implement.

"Mr. President," Solomon began reluctantly, "I have great respect for your leadership, and I thank you for your interest in my opinion. But I hope you will understand that it is not my place to speak on such matters."

"Solomon, I appreciate your respect for protocol. But I know you are a smart boy with a good mind. Otherwise, you wouldn't be here. I began thinking about this colonization business many years ago, but except for Frederick Douglass, I've never gotten a straight answer from most of the Negro leaders I've discussed it with. I sense they don't like the idea but don't want to alienate me with frank responses. Before I make any final decisions on the matter, I'd like the opinions of other Negroes I know and trust. I want your opinion, and whatever it is, I won't hold it against you.

Although Solomon took the president at his word, he had no idea about Seward. But nonetheless, with his scissors and comb still in hand, he turned to face both men, threw caution to the wind, and began speaking his mind.

> Mr. President, you speak of 'A fresh start.' When people like me and my forefathers were brought to this country, we got a fresh start that none of us wanted or expected. We've worked, fought, bled, and died to build America. Some of us built this very house we're in right now, but never earned a cent for our hard labor. I'm guessing that we have worked and sweated even harder than the people that brought us here in chains. I'm also guessing that we've been here longer than many of those who now own everything and rule us with the lash.

> Now that some of us are seeing the possibility of improving our lives here, why would we want to go somewhere else and try to start over? We can't go back to where we came from. We don't even know where that is anymore. We don't know our old languages or even our old names. After generations of enslaver-rape, our bodies are no longer the same. There's nothing for us to go back to. And it will be the same in any new place we might try to make what you call a fresh start. Everything I've ever heard about the movement to colonize in Liberia has been a disaster.

> Regardless of the many obstacles we have faced, my family is proud of what we have accomplished here in America. It's an investment I don't plan to walk away from. With all due respect, Mr. President, and Mr. Secretary, I'm not the least bit interested in any colonization.

Surprised by Solomon's polite but passionate and articulate response, the president pushed back.

"So, because of your desire to remain in America and protect the few gains you have made, you're willing to continue to put up with all the cruel and vicious mistreatment you face in this country?"

"It's true, I want to stay," Solomon answered. "But I'm not willing to put up with ill-treatment forever.

"Yes, I want to protect the gains I have made. But I don't turn a blind eye to racism either. Under your leadership, many people of color are fighting and dying to eliminate the scourge of slavery. If we can someday see the end of this horrible stain on America, that's progress. Then we can move on and fight for other goals, like the right to vote. It won't be easy, but we've got too much invested here to run away from the battle."

"So, for argument's sake," the president responded, "let's say that colonization is a bad idea that should be forgotten. Then what is to be done with the Negro? What would people like you have the president do?"

"Provide justice," Solomon responded, after pausing to recover and collect himself from the powerful emotions that had suddenly and uncharacteristically swept over him.

"But I'm not sure what that justice would be," he continued. "Most of those who brought us to this land in chains are long gone. Although you can't punish a man for crimes committed by his father, you can punish those who continue the crimes today. And it is a fact that no matter how this war ends, great fortunes have been made from slavery. Those fortunes get passed down to people who will continue to live very well whether or not slavery is ever ended. For every white man that has benefited from the spoils of slavery, there are many more slaves and former slaves who still live lives of poverty, pain and suffering.

"So, Mr. President, my hope is that you will fight and win the war. And that you will extend emancipation so that the enslaved are freed in all US states, whether or not in the Confederacy. Many are confused as to why the Emancipation Proclamation freed only slaves in Confederate States. People understand that you want to punish the Confederacy by taking away their slave labor. But don't the enslaved in Union states deserve the same compassion?"

Solomon paused. "With all due respect, Mr. President, perhaps I should stop here."

"Not unless you've spoken your mind," Lincoln answered. "I want to hear all you have to say."

Solomon breathed deeply but said no more, a million thoughts racing through his mind. How could this man not know that emancipation means everyone being set *completely* free, not some partially freed, Solomon puzzled. Was it his place to tell the President of the United States that Negroes see emancipation as a white man's game; white men in Southern states having their slaves taken away as punishment for secession while white men in the North getting to keep theirs as a reward for remaining loyal to the Union? Was it a barber's place to remind the president that if colonization proceeded, Negroes would be the real losers? Slaves from the South would be pushed out of their country of birth, the one they built up from almost nothing, while slaves in the North would remain in bondage until they too were kicked out. Freedmen who worked hard to buy their freedom or who risked their lives to escape slavery would also be required to leave.

Despite his fondness and respect for Lincoln, Solomon was well aware of growing suspicions within the black community about the legitimacy and real purpose of emancipation. If the initiative was truly a fraud perpetrated by the white man, then it followed that Lincoln was the main perpetrator of the fraud. Unwilling to jeopardize the favored position he enjoyed with the president by confronting him with discussion of such negative public perceptions, Solomon changed course, and finally responded: "Mr. President, maybe the issue is not 'What should be done with the Negro?' Perhaps the real question is 'How can the Negro finally get some justice right here where most of us were born?' and 'What will America do to rebuild itself without free labor?'"

Lincoln listened patiently and waited for Solomon to finish his comments before responding.

"Well, I asked for your frank opinion, and I got it," the president finally replied. "It wasn't what I expected, but I believe you spoke from the heart, and I appreciate your forthrightness. You have given me much food for thought."

"Thank you for hearing me out," Solomon replied. "I truly appreciate it, and hope I haven't said too much."

V

Douglass

Power concedes nothing without a demand. It never did and it never will.

Frederick Douglass

Abraham Lincoln first met Frederick Douglass on August 10, 1863, when the fiery abolitionist pushed his way up the White House stairs past a line of angry white office seekers waiting to see the president. Although they had never previously met face to face, the two knew each other well. From a distance, they had long shared a complicated and often contentious relationship. Angered by Lincoln's support of colonization efforts to displace free Negroes, Douglass had frequently criticized the president. Though he had disparaged Lincoln's slow movement to emancipation, Douglass began to respect and appreciate the president after his Emancipation Proclamation that same year. In *Douglass' Monthly*, he wrote:

> Abraham Lincoln... in his own peculiar, cautious, forbearing and hesitating way, slow, but we hope sure, has, while the loyal heart was near breaking with despair, proclaimed and declared: That on the First of January, in the Year of Our Lord One Thousand, Eight Hundred and Sixty-three, All Persons Held as Slaves

Within Any State or Any Designated Part of a State, The People Whereof Shall Then be in Rebellion Against the United States, Shall be Thenceforward and Forever Free.

Abraham Lincoln may be slow, Abraham Lincoln may desire peace even at the price of leaving our terrible national sore untouched, to fester on for generations, but Abraham Lincoln is not the man to reconsider, retract and contradict words and purposes solemnly proclaimed over his official signature."

Given their unusually distinctive but strangely similar origins of deprivation, strength, and resilience, it is no surprise that the two leaders would come to enjoy deep mutual respect and friendship. Both had grown up in extremely challenging circumstances. Douglass, the bold abolitionist leader and escaped slave had taught himself to read and write by studying wordbooks recovered from the trash of his mistress, and by copying the letters of the names carved into boats on which he worked in the shipyard of his master. Lincoln, born impoverished on a country farm, had ascended to the presidency despite having received no more than one year of formal education. Despite his minimal schooling and the influence of an illiterate father who thought of education as foolish idling, Lincoln trained himself with donated books. Many of his study materials were provided by his also-illiterate stepmother who had saved them from her late husband's collection.

Born into slavery on a Maryland farm eight years after Lincoln's birth, Frederick Augustus Washington Bailey lived under the care of his grandmother after his own mother, Harriet Bailey, was hired out to another nearby farm. He rarely saw Harriet and never knew his exact birthdate. His father was likely the white man who owned his mother. During his childhood, Frederick was moved frequently, and at six, he was sent to be a house slave and playmate of the twelve-year-old son of a former Maryland governor. The privileged older boy took a liking to his young companion and began teaching him how to read and speak standard English.

At age eight, Frederick was again sent to new owners in Baltimore, where as a "city slave," he enjoyed better meals and slept in a bed rather than on the dirt floors he had always known. Now running errands on the streets of a large city, young "Freddy" was exposed to a cosmopolitan environment in which many Negroes were freedmen. Recognizing his intelligence and eagerness to learn, his new mistress helped him with his reading and mastery of English until her husband rebuked her with a warning that learning would do the young slave no good and instead might make him restless and eager to escape.

For the next eight years, Frederick would continue to surreptitiously study and learn until he was unexpectedly sent back to Maryland farm country to work one year for Edward Covey, a local farmer known for his skills in breaking young Negro slaves. Now seventeen, Frederick endured long hours working the fields. He also suffered repeated thrashings until the consequential moment on a hot August day when the now-strapping bondsman decided he would no longer submit to his master's beatings. When Covey attempted to bind him for punishment, Frederick resisted. The two engaged in a brutal struggle, grappling for more than an hour with Frederick taking pains to protect himself while not injuring Covey.

When his adversary summoned help, Frederick kicked and incapacitated a responding bondsman while continuing to battle Covey. Another slave who had also been sent to Covey to be broken, refused to assist, telling him that he had been sent to work on the plantation, not subdue other slaves.

Fought to a standstill and unable to enlist help, Covey ended the confrontation. "Go back to work," he ordered Frederick, adding, "I would not have whipped you half so much as I have had you not resisted."

When Covey failed to report to the local constable that a slave had raised his hand to a white man, a capital offense in many cases, Frederick realized that if Covey had reported him, his reputation as a slave breaker would suffer. Himself having been broken, the slaver would never again attempt to punish Frederick who now thought of himself as a free man. It would not be much longer until he escaped to freedom, adopting the new name, Frederick Douglass.

Abraham Lincoln's background had also been challenging, even if not as difficult as Douglass's. Although born white and free, in his early years, he lived the life of an indentured servant under a cold and willful taskmaster of a father who put him to work at age eight on the family farm and hired him out to neighboring farms, keeping the wages earned by his son. At age twenty-one, after moving with his family from Kentucky to Illinois and helping his father build a new log cabin, Lincoln set out on his own. He initially settled in the Illinois river town of Salem, where he took a job as a clerk in a local store. He lodged in the attic above the store and slept on a cot. Six years later, after brief service in a local volunteer militia, he ran for but lost a race for a seat on the Illinois General Assembly. After a series of unsuccessful business ventures, Lincoln began serving as a legal advocate despite having no legal training. In 1836, the now-popular future president ran for and finally won his first elected political office, a seat on the Illinois Legislature.

During the early years of the war, Douglass had become a strong advocate for black military enlistment. Although ex-slaves were now serving unofficially with the US military, there was widespread concern among senior officers about the courage and intelligence of colored troops. President Lincoln shared those concerns and worried that white troops would refuse to serve with them. Even though Negro enlistment was low, several all-colored army regiments had been formed.

Despite his continuing advocacy for black military enlistment, Douglass began to publicly express his reservations about the changes in their status that could be expected by people of color after a war to end slavery. In public addresses and newspaper articles, he enumerated the many passing events that had shaken, but not destroyed, his faith that the war would have a positive outcome for people of color and that contributions of Negro troops would be appreciated.

Douglass voiced concerns about Secretary of State Seward's instruction to US ministers and ambassadors to inform the governments with which they interfaced that: "Terminate however it might, the status of no people of the United States would be changed by the rebellion—that the slaves would be slaves still, and that the masters would be masters still." He spoke with alarm about the warning of Generals McClellan and Fremont to slaves that: "If any attempt was made by them to gain their freedom it would be suppressed with an iron hand."

Among the many other issues that troubled him, Douglass denounced the Missouri governor's withdrawal of the state's Emancipation Proclamation, the return of slaves to their masters by Union soldiers, and the assignment of soldiers to Virginia farmhouses to protect the masters in holding their slaves. He was particularly critical of Lincoln's assertion to the Negro that "he was the cause of the war."

But despite these concerns, Douglass continued to publicly state his belief that the mission of the war was the liberation of the slave and the salvation of the Union. He reproached the North that "they fought the rebels with only one hand, when they might strike more effectively with two—that they fought with their soft white hand, while they kept their black iron hand chained and helpless behind them—that they fought the effect, while they protected the cause of slavery, and that the Union cause would never prosper until the war assumed an antislavery attitude, and the Negro was enlisted on the loyal side."

Black men joined the army in greater numbers after President Lincoln encouraged it as part of the Emancipation Proclamation. Following the proclamation and a request from Secretary of War Edwin Stanton that he work, as a commissioned assistant adjutant, to increase colored enlistment in the South, Douglass focused his attention on recruiting black soldiers and securing equal pay and treatment for all servicemen regardless of color. He even recruited his sons, Charles and

Lewis, to join the Fifty-Fourth Massachusetts Infantry Regiment. Two months after the proclamation, forty-five-year-old Douglass addressed a Rochester, New York audience on March 2, 1863, with his *Men of Color to Arms!* words of encouragement:

> When first the rebel cannon shattered the walls of Sumter and drove away its starving garrison, I predicted that the war then and there inaugurated would not be fought out entirely by white men. Every month's experience during these dreary years has confirmed that opinion. A war undertaken and brazenly carried on for the perpetual enslavement of colored men, calls logically and loudly for colored men to help suppress it.... I have implored the imperiled nation to unchain against her foes, her powerful black hand. Slowly and reluctantly that appeal is beginning to be heeded.

To all men of color, not just those in the audience, Douglass issued an urgent challenge:

> ... by all the ties of blood and identity which make us one with the brave black men now fighting our battles in Louisiana and in South Carolina, I urge you to fly to arms, and smite with death the power that would bury the government and your liberty in the same hopeless grave.

But only five months later in a letter to Major George L. Stearns, his main interface with the army, Douglass expressed new concerns. "When I plead for recruits," he explained, I want to do it with all my heart, without qualification. I cannot do that now. The impression settles upon me that that colored men have much overrated the enlightenment, justice, and generosity of our rulers in Washington. In my humble way, I have contributed to that somewhat false estimate." Douglass went on to explain that when the idea of raising colored troops was first suggested, the plan for them was to garrison forts and arsenals in the South. Black troops were considered more suited than whites to the extremely warm temperatures in Southern installations.

The advantages of this arrangement were to be that the spirit of white troops would not be wasted in the monotonous activities of fort support and maintenance, the health of white troops would be preserved by not subjecting them to high temperatures for long periods, and black troops would receive sound military training and remain safe from capture by rebels who had avowed their intention to enslave and slaughter them. Douglas went on to explain that thus far, no black troops had been placed in charge of holding any army fortifications. They thus remained exposed to capture and assassination in violation of war codes. Many black Union troops held prisoner by rebel forces were never again heard from or offered in Confederate prisoner trades.

As he was an avowed abolitionist who, before his military service, had established an Underground Railroad station in his hometown of Bedford, Massachusetts, Stearns listened sympathetically to Douglass's entreaties. When he suggested that Douglass's concerns be expressed directly to President Lincoln, a meeting was arranged.

Despite earlier disagreements, when they finally met, Lincoln received Douglass cordially. The outspoken ex-slave, now a world-renowned orator and statesman, began the meeting by thanking the president for finally extending protection to colored soldiers with his recently issued retaliatory order.

Recognizing that the brilliant, radical pragmatist sitting across from him that morning might help him to ensure the nation's survival, Lincoln took pains to explain that, on questions of slavery and emancipation, he was not vacillating and wavering as had been charged by many, including Douglass. What the public was witnessing, he claimed, was steady, if at times slow, progress rather than indecision. An example was the retaliatory order Douglass had just thanked him for, but that many had criticized him for foot-dragging in its issuance. He believed that if he had acted too soon, before Confederates announced their intention to capitally punish black soldiers, many of his critics might complain: "Ah! We thought it would come to this: White men are to be killed for Negroes."

Encouraged by Lincoln's comments, Douglass segued to his black enlistment initiative, referencing his recent *Men of Color to Arms* address. He once again implored the president to improve the treatment of colored soldiers and provided several examples of Union misconduct directed toward troops of color. When Lincoln confirmed Douglass's military appointment as an *Assistant Adjutant Officer* and signed the commission order, Douglass came away from the meeting feeling that the president was a trustworthy man whose word was his bond. He was encouraged that the two had shared an honest and mutually respectful communication.

Douglass was not in Pennsylvania later that year to hear the president's memorable Gettysburg Address. But he was deeply inspired with Lincoln's reference to the proposition that all men are created equal; an unachieved goal set by the founding fathers eighty-seven earlier. He was struck by the public recognition of what had long been a reality for Negroes in America, that the nation had been founded on a false premise. Acknowledging that the goal of equality was "unfinished work" and "a great task remaining before us," the president resolved that "...this nation, under God, shall have a new birth of freedom—and that government of the people, by the people, shall not perish from the earth."

Douglass was energized and uplifted by the president's pledge that, through the painful sacrifices of war, the nation would be reborn to finally achieve the lofty goals established by the founders. It was inconceivable to him that a few years later, after the war was won, the reconstruction of the nation might be overthrown and that, once again, citizens of color would be left wondering whether the goals of equality for all could ever be achieved.

Douglass was invited back to the White House on August 19 of the following year to discuss Lincoln's emancipation efforts. Specifically, the president sought advice on how to further induce slaves in rebel states to come within the federal lines. He wanted to increase the number of former slaves who would remain free even if he was not reelected that fall. Concerned about the upcoming election, Lincoln thought the move might improve his prospects for victory. No longer adversaries, the two men had developed a mutual respect and frequently exchanged advice and suggestions. Douglass would later comment in his autobiography: "What Lincoln said on this day showed a deeper moral conviction against slavery than I had ever before seen in anything spoken or written by him."

In March of 1865, at his second inauguration one month before his assassination, Lincoln would deliver an address that Douglass and many others consider his finest; better even than his Emancipation Proclamation. On this occasion, he would address the institution of slavery as a cause of the Civil War in a more insightful and compelling manner than ever before. In his first inaugural address he had spoken of how the war was being fought to preserve the Union:

> We didn't go into the war to put down slavery, but to put the flag back, and to act differently at this moment, would, I have no doubt, not only weaken our cause but smack of bad faith; for I never should have had votes enough to send me here if the people had supposed I should try to use my power to upset slavery.

In his second inauguration address, the president's insights would be deeper and his assessments more accurate. In a riveting six-minute speech to a large, integrated audience that included Douglass, he evoked a "call and response" interaction with black listeners when he finally acknowledged that slavery was at the root of the rebellion:

> Both the North and the South read the same Bible and pray to the same God; and each invokes His aid against the other. It may seem strange that any men should dare ask a just God's assistance

in wringing their bread from the sweat of the other men's faces; but let us judge not that we be not judged.

Fondly do we hope—fervently do we pray—that this mighty scourge of war may speedily pass away. Yet if God wills that it continue until all the wealth piled by the bond-man's two hundred fifty years of unrequited toil shall be sunk, and until every drop of blood drawn with the lash, shall be paid by another drawn with the sword...so still it must be said "the judgments of the Lord are true and righteous altogether."

Douglass would meet with Lincoln one last time after this speech. Douglass had heard the address and wanted to visit with the president at the White House to congratulate his inaugural victory. Initially prevented from entering because of his color, when Douglass finally was allowed into the East Room, the president greeted him warmly. "I am glad to see you," Lincoln told him. "I saw you in the crowd to-day, listening to my inaugural address...Douglass; there is no man in the country whose opinion I value more than yours. I want to know what you think of it." Douglass responded, simply, "Mr. Lincoln, that was a sacred effort." Douglass would always treasure the memory of how he, a former slave, and an American president had built a friendship that allowed them to share such a moment.

Later, in an 1876 speech given during the unveiling of the Freedman's Monument in the nation's capital, Douglass would encapsulate his admiration and fondness for the fallen leader:

Abraham Lincoln was not, in the fullest sense of the word, either our man or our model...He was preeminently the white man's President, entirely devoted to the welfare of white men... though the Union was more to him than our freedom or our future, under his wise and beneficent rule we saw ourselves gradually lifted from the depths of slavery to the heights of liberty and manhood.

VI

Dangerous Liaisons

*Once the black man gets upon his person, the brass
letters, U.S., let him get an eagle on his button, and a
musket on his shoulder and bullets in his pocket,
there is no power on earth that can deny that he has
earned the right to citizenship.*

Frederick Douglass

On July 3, 1860, one year after Solomon's rescue of the missing boys kidnapped by Blackbirders in Columbus and one year before the first shot of the Civil War, John Surratt stood before a stately mansion in Baltimore's *Monument Square* preparing to begin a life-altering experience of his own. The Maryland College student, born the same year as Solomon, was accompanied by his friend and fellow Baltimorean, John Wilkes Booth.

A popular stage actor, Booth had invited him to take the vows of membership in the *Knights of the Golden Circle,* a militant secret society focused on preserving slavery in the US and expanding it from current slaveholding states into parts of Mexico, Central America, and the West Indies. In the early days of the run-up to the Civil War, the Knights had been rapidly building their membership to support the Southern states' plan to secede from the Union. Booth and other candidates like him were attracted by the organization's pro-slavery goals which were to expand the nation southward and protect constitutional liberties from assaults by abolitionists and black republicans. Although Booth had been initiated into the society the previous year, in accordance with his KGC vows, he never publicly acknowledged his membership. Neither would Surratt. In accordance with the Circle's strict secrecy policy, the two would not even acknowledge their friendship until they were formally introduced years later.

The Knights were a decentralized network with regional commanders in mostly Southern states. These leaders were usually backed by friendly Southern newspaper editors and politicians. In late 1860, these state commanders had shifted their focus from colonization of free Negroes in destinations outside the US to supporting radical governors in their drive toward secession. Through public meetings and political action, they promoted rebellion and attempted to intimidate opposing voices into silence.

As the organization became more widely known, there was pushback, not only from abolitionists but also from disaffected members who published exposés of scandals involving present and past government officials who supported secession. They charged that Lincoln's predecessor, James Buchanan, and other Southern-rights members of the cabinet were KGC members. Vice President John Breckinridge and Secretary of War John Floyd were named, and claims were made that the Knights were behind a Southern conspiracy to capture federal forts and arsenals in the South and prevent Lincoln's inauguration. It was disclosed that Floyd had surreptitiously moved more than one hundred Columbiads, the Union's most powerful artillery piece, to Southern forts under construction. When a committee of outraged citizens of Pittsburgh, the city where the giant guns were manufactured, sent a telegram to President Buchannan that the weapons would soon be sent to Mississippi, not their original intended destination, the president reluctantly intervened, and Floyd was soon relieved of his position.

Such scandals did not dissuade passionate Southern supporters like Booth from KGC membership, but instead inflamed them and made them even more eager to join. The young actor would soon begin using his KGC connections to smuggle quinine and other drugs to the Confederacy.

From the outside, the large mansion in Baltimore's *Monument Square* had the appearance of a fashionable dwelling. The arrival of the two companions at twelve noon fit into the normal daytime flow of activities in the wealthy neighborhood, as late-night meetings during preparations for the war might have aroused suspicions among neighbors. Booth led his friend up the entry steps, and with a slight push, the ornate front door flew open. Inside they faced a second door, half glass and covered on the inside with heavy lace curtains. After signaling Surratt to maintain strict silence, Booth tapped the glass panel and was quickly answered with a similar tapping from an unseen party on the other side of the glass. A second tapping by Booth caused the inner door to swing open revealing no trace of how or by whom entry was provided.

In eerie silence, the two climbed a stairway at the far end of the room. At the top of the steps, Booth exchanged another sequence of signal knocks that caused a heavy wood door to open, providing them entry into a dark room. Surratt shuddered as the door closed behind them, and he felt the sharp point of a weapon pressed against his chest. He labored to maintain his composure when he heard the ominous sound of a deep voice before him.

"Those who would pass here must face both fire and steel!" the voice announced.

"We are willing to face both for liberty," Booth responded.

"It shall be ours," the voice replied. "Pass!"

Surratt's hand was taken, and he was led, in darkness, down a long hallway to another heavy door which swung wide open as he approached.

"Advance," said the voice, and Surratt stepped into a large room. The door closed behind him, and he was now alone, Booth having disappeared somewhere along the way.

This room was comfortably furnished, and its several windows allowed bright sunlight to stream in. A rich wallpaper featured a pattern of gold rings, and throughout the room there hung life-sized portraits of famous Southern leaders such as John C. Calhoun, Franklin Pierce, and Jefferson Davis. The room's blue ceiling was ornamented with a large gold circle and an elaborate wedding cake chandelier was suspended from its center.

After a long and nervous wait, the curtains suddenly and mysteriously dropped, leaving the room completely dark. Surratt's hands were seized, and a blindfold was placed over his eyes. As he was led down yet another long hall, several more doors opened before him and closed behind him. He was stopped at a final door where his shirt was ripped open to expose his bare chest. Another sequence of signal knocks was exchanged, and a question posed from within.

"Who comes here?"

"One who is true to our cause," Booth replied, once again accompanying Surratt.

"How is he known to be true?" the questioner asked.

"By the recommendation of a tried knight," came the reply.

"He can then be trusted?" the questioner persisted.

"Such is our belief."

"But if he should fail and betray us, what then?" The final question.

"He will learn the penalty soon enough." The response.

"Then advance!"

After he was led forward a few steps, Surratt once again felt the contact of cold steel and the point of a sharp weapon against his chest. In a slow and measured tone, another voice announced:

"Those who would pass here must face both fire and steel. Are you willing to do so?"

After answering in the affirmative, Surratt was told to kneel on a cushion and directed to repeat, word for word, an oath recited to him as one of his hands was placed on an open book and the other on some kind of a cold object.

His obligation completed, Surratt was instructed to remember every word he had uttered, and to not forget the penalty for disclosing any of what he might learn or for betraying the names of anyone in the organization. He was advised that he was now obligated to carry out all orders given him by the Circle, and that he should be ready to assist all brother-knights, even at the risk of his own death.

"Are you willing to abide by this obligation?" asked the voice.

Before he could answer, the voice continued: "Brother knights! Recall to the mind of him who now kneels here, the penalty of betrayal, either by sign, word, or deed."

In a thunderous response, a hundred or more voices hissed, whispered, and shouted:

"Death! Death! Death!"

"It is well," said the voice, finally. "Proceed! Show him all."

As a loud chorus of voices repeated the words and his blindfold was removed, Surratt felt many sharp points pressed against his bare chest. His eyes slowly adjusting to the now brightly sunlit room, he became aware that he was surrounded by a throng of armed men covered with coats of mail similar to the armor worn by medieval knights. Red and white feathers adorned their helmets, and their swords all touched his chest. He suddenly realized that he faced an altar, that his left hand was placed on an open Bible and his right on the face of a corpse! He shuddered with revulsion as he glanced toward the floor and realized he was kneeling on the chest of another corpse!

Barely able to control his shock at the bizarre and gruesome ceremony, Surratt was ushered into an adjoining anteroom where he was given the KGC signs, grips, and passwords that allowed Knights to recognize each other. He was then allowed to sit in solitude and contemplate his initiation. A short while later, he was joined by Booth who was back in street clothing.

"Congratulations, my worthy fellow knight," Booth greeted him. "Collect yourself and let us get back to the crisis facing our country. There is much work to be done."

By the fall of 1860, attitudes had hardened among Southerners bent on secession. Their bitterness and hatred of the Union had reached the breaking point as the presidential elections approached. The final straw for them was the November election of Abraham Lincoln. The day after his election, South Carolina raised the flag of secession, and in December, it left the Union, the first of the Southern states to do so. In February of 1861, several other states followed to form the Confederacy. By then, Jefferson Davis had been installed as its president and Lincoln was preparing to travel to Washington for his own inauguration.

As the Southern states were exiting the Union, John Surratt was called on by Booth who had recently returned from Richmond where he had met with several influential Confederate leaders. Surratt had been working diligently but unsuccessfully with his new fellow Knights trying to influence his home state of Maryland to join the secession. Booth had been assigned an important mission the Southerners believed was key to their success: delaying or preventing Lincoln's presidential party from reaching Washington for his March inauguration. They had resolved that the Northern Railsplitter could never be installed as president in a city where Southerners had once directed the affairs of the nation. Through their KGC network, they believed they had control of all Southern arsenals and were convinced they had the resources to prevent Lincoln from taking office. They were confident they could capture the Capital at any time but decided to delay their siege until Lincoln returned so that they could capture him along with the city.

Booth asked Surratt to join him in leading the mission. Working through the Knights with a network of Confederate contracts, Booth had already devised an action plan. He was motivated by the prospect that he and Surratt might soon proclaim to the Confederacy that the city of Washington was hers and, if desired, that it could be designated Capital of the Confederacy.

In early February, Lincoln left his hometown of Springfield Ohio on a twelve-day whistle-stop train excursion that would end in the District of Columbia in time for his March 4 inauguration. The trip would provide him with an opportunity to speak at several northern cities along the way. The first overnight event in Indianapolis went well, but as the presidential party prepared to leave Cincinnati, the site of the second event, a railway attendant discovered a carpet bag under Lincoln's seat in the presidential car. Inside the bag a grenade was discovered that was set to explode with a force that would have destroyed the entire car. Although the perpetrator was never caught or even identified, it was clear that the president-elect was in mortal danger and that Confederate intelligence was tracking his movement. Lincoln and his advisors did not yet fully understand the extent to which KCG spies were providing critical intelligence.

Through these agents, Booth had learned that after stops in Pennsylvania, the president-elect's train route would take him through Baltimore and across Gunpowder Bridge, an old, covered structure that would provide an excellent opportunity for an interception. With the help of many of the knights present at Surratt's initiation, Booth's plan was to stop the train at the bridge, extract Lincoln and Vice President-elect Hamlin and quickly move them to a secure location before bodyguards or a security team could react. There they would be held for ransom or possibly assassination.

Surratt was not comfortable with Booth's plan. Although he admired his fellow knight's boldness and daring, he also saw Booth as a flawed crusader and knew him to be an impulsive ladies' man frequently in and out of casual relationships. The last few times he had seen him, Booth had been accompanied by a new woman who talked to him in an overbearing manner and always seemed to be carefully observing his every move and word. If she had learned of his plan and revealed it to Northerners, the resulting situation would have been an embarrassing failure for the South that would have been reported extensively in newspapers.

Surratt's suspicions were correct. Although, like Booth, he was more the passionate pro-South zealot than cool-headed tactical planner, he was correct in fearing that Union Intelligence might have discovered Booth's plan.

Lincoln had been advised of the plot and had completely changed his travel plans. His speaking engagement and a reception planned for that evening were cancelled. Telegraph lines from Harrisburg to Baltimore were temporarily disconnected, and Lincoln returned to Philadelphia on a special one-car train. Hidden under an old fedora and an overcoat unlike anything he might normally wear, the president-elect boarded a night train to Baltimore accompanied by a single bodyguard and a Pinkerton agent. Upon arrival, he immediately boarded a Washington-bound train, and was safely in Washington a few hours later. He arrived at the capitol close to the time he and his party had been expected to reach Baltimore. Once again, Lincoln had dodged a bullet.

Predictably, newspapers in the South criticized Lincoln's "cowardice," while those in the North ridiculed Southern plotters for their ineptness. The self-avowed Black Republican was relieved to have made it to his inauguration and was beginning to understand that, without more attention to his security, he might not survive his presidential term.

Despite two close calls, once he was sworn in, settled into the White House, and consumed with wartime leadership duties, personal security became less of a concern to the busy president. Holding together the Union and prosecuting a difficult war occupied almost all his waking thoughts. But from time to time, he sought relief.

Often described as shy and melancholy, the beleaguered leader showed a gregarious and friendly side by frequently hosting open house events during which the White House was open to the public. In those moments he could engage in informal chats with citizens. He fondly referred to these encounters as his *public opinion baths*. The format was simple; at appointed times, usually in the morning, the gates to the White House were opened and visitors were allowed to queue up at the front door and in a hallway leading up to a large sitting room at the front of the residence. Sitting at a writing table piled high with documents, the walls around the room covered with maps, and a window looking out to the Potomac, the president received guests not by rank or importance, but in the form of a lottery conducted by ushers. He would politely greet each visitor and patiently listen to their comments or requests. After asking a few questions or responding to those of his guest, the president would inform the visitor of the actions that would be taken by him or one of his staff. Not every guest could be seen in each open house session, and in some cases, many visits and many hours in line were required before the busy leader could be seen. But, for the most part, the public appreciated the president's gesture and the opportunity he offered citizens to receive personal attention.

Lincoln continued his open houses throughout his first term. Upon his arrival with the Light Guard in late 1863, Solomon served on White House guard duty for several of these events. On one occasion as he and one of the other guards prepared to close the doors at the end of the open house, the president waved them off. Lincoln approached two women, the only guests remaining in the meeting room, and asked what he could do for them. They answered that they had come to request consideration for two men imprisoned for resisting the draft in Western Pennsylvania. The elder of the two women was the mother of one man, the younger, the wife of the other. When the president asked for their petition, they explained that they couldn't write and had no money to have one written.

Lincoln summoned Assistant Secretary of War Charles Dana and requested him to bring a list of Western Pennsylvanians in jail for draft evasion. After reviewing the list, he instructed Dana to draw up an order setting them all free. When the younger woman attempted to kneel in appreciation, the president told her: "Don't kneel to me but thank God...." With tears in her eyes as she took the president's hand, her older companion said: "Good-bye, Mr. Lincoln. I shall probably never see you again until we meet in heaven." Deeply moved, Lincoln walked the two to the door and responded, "I am afraid that with all my troubles, I shall never get to the resting-place you speak of; but if I do, I am sure I shall find you. That you wish me to get there is, I do believe, the best wish you could make for me."

Solomon had always known that when Lincoln's late barber had been first hired at Treasury, it had been done at the president's urging. Secretary Chase had hired William as a clerk, a position he held in name only as his real duties involved tending to the Treasury Building furnace. When he sensed the time was right, Solomon asked the president about the possibility that he might take over William's clerk position. But instead of working as a laborer and tending the furnace, he asked that he be allowed to actively perform clerk duties in the Treasury Department. Of course, he would continue his barbering services for the president.

When Solomon mentioned his earlier conversations with Secretary Chase, the president immediately drafted a letter to the Treasury Department requesting that Solomon be given the position opened when William died.

Treasury Department
Office of the Secretary
Washington, D.C.

January 28, 1864

This boy says he knows Secretary Chase and would like to have the place made vacant by William Johnson's death. I believe he is a good boy, and I should be glad for him to have the place if it is still vacant.

(signed) A. Lincoln

The day after the president sent his request, Solomon was hired as a messenger in the Treasury Department at a salary of six hundred dollars per year. He was instructed, by a letter from the Assistant Secretary of the Treasury, that he was to begin work immediately. Because he was a quartermaster employee of the Light Guard and not "regular army" as were the white guardsmen, Solomon was able to quickly transition out of his military duties.

VII

The Lost Cause

In my opinion, the Religion that sets men to rebel and fight against their government, because, as they think, that government does not sufficiently help some men to eat their bread on the sweat of other men's faces, is not the sort of Religion upon which people can get to heaven!

Abraham Lincoln

In recent weeks, the president had not been himself. Solomon had noticed his increasing agitation as the summer months began, both in his uncharacteristically animated conversation with certain cabinet members during haircuts or shaves, and in the frequency and seeming urgency of his daily visits to the War Building. In the spring, Lincoln had finally agreed to be accompanied by a guard on his walks. But at times, he would make the trek alone. During the past week, Solomon had been working White House evening guard duty and had twice spotted the president walking briskly to the War Building by himself.

Solomon assumed that the president was troubled, not only by the continuing ebb and flow of a bloody war that had split the nation politically, militarily, and spiritually, but also by the possibility of a defeat in the fall election of 1864. He learned the real cause of the tension later that week when he was called to the White House to shave the president and arrived to find him in the middle of an animated discussion about the war and the recent Battle of Atlanta with his Secretary of War, Edwin Stanton. To Solomon's surprise, the two continued their military strategy session without interruption as he began his work. He had always assumed that presidential war discussions would only involve top officials and would be top secret.

Although Solomon had missed the early part of their conversation, it was clear the president was concerned that war weariness in the North was diminishing his chances for a November election victory. The president and the secretary also agreed that the longer the outgunned and outmanned Confederacy was allowed to continue the fight, the greater the chance they might pull off an upset. Early in 1864, Lincoln had taken the first step in breaking the stalemate when he gave future president Ulysses Grant command of all the Armies of the United States and announced his appointment as General-in-Chief. Now a lieutenant general, the highest grade in the United States Army, Grant assigned General William Sherman to lead an offensive campaign deep into Confederate territory in hopes of bringing the war to an end.

The *Atlanta Campaign* would be a series of nine major battles and numerous smaller actions fought in the Western Theater of the Civil War between May and September. The Western Theater encompassed major military operations in the states of Alabama, Georgia, Florida, Mississippi, North Carolina, Kentucky, South Carolina, Tennessee, and Louisiana east of the Mississippi River. Grant's strategy involved simultaneous engagements against several Confederate armies to prevent enemy units from reinforcing each other. The Battle of Atlanta, the most important of the nine engagements, would be aimed at capturing Atlanta and destroying one of the Confederacy's main railroad, supply, and manufacturing centers. As Atlanta was positioned just south of Richmond, Virginia, the Confederate capital, Grant and Sherman believed the fall of Atlanta would destabilize the Confederacy and end the war.

As Solomon proceeded with the president's shave, Stanton reported that the Atlanta engagement had been launched southeast of Atlanta two days earlier, on July 22, when Major General William T. Sherman led more than 100,000 union troops in the assault and capture of the railway center of Atlanta. Sherman's soldiers faced the Confederate Army of Tennessee under the command of General John Bell Hood. Although Hood commanded less than 70,000 troops, he took advantage of the mountainous, woody terrain of northwestern Georgia to hold off Sherman's forces. But Sherman faced additional challenges in battling Hood's troops. As Western Theater Commander with several other military commitments, he had to shuttle troops between the Atlanta campaign and the protection of the Western Atlantic Railroad to ensure that its important supply line remained open.

In a savage, all-day battle, the Union suffered more than 3,700 casualties. Although the Confederate casualties numbered some 5,500, a serious blow for their already depleted army, they still held Atlanta. Union Major General James B. McPherson was killed in the battle, and among the many other casualties that day, Confederate Major General William H. T. Walker was also killed when he was shot from his horse by a Union sharpshooter. The Union attack and associated losses split the Confederate forces as had been done the previous year in a decisive victory at Vicksburg, Mississippi which many believed was a turning point in the war.

The presidential briefing ended as Lincoln's shave was completed. As he applied after-shave lotion, Solomon sensed the president's relief at having received a positive report at such a critical point in the war. Solomon was also uplifted by the good news. He was touched that although he served only as the president's barber, the beleaguered leader still thought of him as a Union soldier who might enjoy hearing good news that he could share with other members of his Light Guard unit.

On August 31, Sherman's army captured the railroad track from Macon, Georgia, thereby completely severing the enemy's supply lines. Confederate General John Hood pulled his troops out of Atlanta the next day. As he left, he destroyed supply depots and set fire to eighty-one loaded ammunition cars to prevent them from falling into Union hands. Two days later, Mayor James Calhoun surrendered the city, asking Union officials for "protection to non-combatants and private property."

The following week, General Sherman ordered all non-military personnel out of Atlanta and established his own headquarters, staying until November 15th. He then launched his memorable *March to the Sea*, a brutal campaign that attacked military and civilian targets alike as his army marched almost 300 miles east of Atlanta to the coastal city of Savannah which surrendered without firing a shot.

The fall of Atlanta raised morale in the North and boosted President Lincoln's political standing, cementing his well-deserved image as a strong wartime leader. In the 1864 election, Democratic challenger and former Union General George McClellan would run a poor campaign and help the president to be reelected by a wide margin, with 212 out of 233 electoral votes.

The devastating assault on Atlanta and Sherman's relentless march would cause long-lasting bitterness and resentment in the postbellum South. Sliding into a state of perpetual victimhood, the Confederacy would view Sherman's march as another element of the overwhelming force it endured as it fought its valiant *Lost Cause*, a heroic war not intended to preserve slavery but to uphold states' rights against a Northern aggression that threatened the Southern way of life.

The Lost Cause would attempt to perpetuate the mythology that slavery had been more benevolent than cruel. Bizarre stories of happy, contented slaves would forever be used to portray the South as more a society of Christian values than the materialistic North. Promoters of the Lost Cause myth maintained that slavery was not the cause of secession and that it would only be a matter of time before the South would have given up slavery by its own choice. They argued that radical abolitionists had agitated unnecessary conflict between the North and the South and maintained that slaves were faithful, happy, and loyal to their masters. Characterizing the South as a land of grace and culture, they argued that the races were united in support of the Southern way of life and that secession was a right granted by the Constitution.

But these representations of a gracious Southern life full of love and respect between beneficent masters and grateful slaves evolved mostly from a nearly defeated secessionist nation attempting to burnish a tainted image. The South's almost saintly claims of a slavery more benevolent than cruel differed sharply from earlier pro-slavery arguments such as the *Cornerstone Speech* of Confederate States of America Vice-President Alexander H. Stephens, in which he invoked biblical scripture to characterize white supremacy and black subordination as the cornerstone upon which the Confederacy was founded:

> Our new government foundations are laid, its cornerstone rests upon the great truth, that the Negro is not equal to the white man; that slavery—subordination to the superior race—is his natural and normal condition. This, our new government, is the first, in the history of the world, based upon this great physical, philosophical, and moral truth.

But even among those who led the insurrection there was no uniform view as to the morality of slavery. In an 1856 letter to his wife several years before the war, Confederate General Robert E. Lee expressed unusual views on Slavery:

> There are few, I believe, in this enlightened age, who will not acknowledge that slavery as an institution is a moral and political evil. It is idle to expatiate on its disadvantages. I think it is a greater evil to the white than to the colored race. While my feelings are strongly enlisted in behalf of the latter, my sympathies

are more deeply engaged for the former. The blacks are immeasurably better off here than in Africa, morally, physically, and socially. The painful discipline they are undergoing is necessary for their further instruction as a race, and will prepare them, I hope, for better things. How long their servitude may be necessary is known and ordered by a merciful Providence.

The victimhood associated with the Lost Cause myth would later lead to an attack on Reconstruction and a drive for the return of white supremacy and the revocation of freedmen rights. The aggressive and violent initiative to reverse the human rights gains of the Civil War would become known as *Redemption,* the efforts of Southern political leaders and white supremacists to undo gains made by the Republican party and black people following the Civil War. W. E. B. Dubois would later describe the slide from Civil War victory and Reconstruction to Redemption as an era in which: "The slave went free; stood a brief moment in the sun; then moved back again toward slavery."

VIII ▌

Treasury

This is our home, and this is our country. Beneath its soil lie bones of our fathers: for it some of them fought, bled, and died. Here we were born and here we will stay.

Paul Robeson

Eager to begin his new challenge, Solomon reported for work at the Treasury Department Friday morning January 29, 1864. He did not enter the building through the stately granite columns framing the north door at 1500 Pennsylvania Avenue, but rather through a heavily guarded southwest corner entrance. Under the protective gaze of a statue of Alexander Hamilton, the first Secretary of the Treasury, Solomon was searched and questioned by troops of the Fifth Massachusetts Regiment before he was permitted entry.

As the Civil War continued to take its toll on the US, the Treasury Building became more than the nation's center of finance. The massive facility had come to represent the strength of the nation in turbulent times. Recent renovations were intended to help it not only withstand the test of time but to also serve as a stronghold of defense against any Confederate incursions into the capital and attempts to seize the treasury. Thus, the Treasury Building had come to serve as not only the hub of the nation's monetary and financial operation, but also as a barricade and barracks for soldiers, a secure site available to the president should the White House come under attack. Treasury officials ensured that armed troops surrounded the building at all times, and they fortified the newly renovated basement so that it could serve as a presidential bunker. They never again wanted to risk capture or destruction of the facility as had twice previously occurred, in 1814 when it was destroyed by British forces, and in 1833 when it was lost through neglect.

After clearing the guard station, Solomon was directed to a small meeting room a few doors from a sumptuous third floor office suite that was being readied for Secretary Chase. There he was received by Assistant Secretary Field who assigned him to the mail section of the Internal Revenue Division. His duties would include handling and moving incoming and outgoing mail pouches, sorting mail, and delivering messages. Since the Treasury was undergoing major renovations, on occasion Solomon would be called upon to assist the plasterers, riggers, stonemasons, and other workers renovating the building.

As he traversed his daily messenger route between Treasury, the White House, the War Department, the Navy Department and the State Department, Solomon observed a variety of governmental functions and came to know many of the assigned department officials and clerical workers. Within Treasury, he became particularly interested in the currency production function.

The 1861 National Currency Act allowed the federal government to begin issuing paper money. Initially, "greenbacks" were printed offsite and then shipped to Treasury where they were separated and hand-signed individually by Treasury workers. To produce hundreds of millions in US notes, a factory-type system was created that required extensive staff and space. But with currency signed by multiple people, there was no single, easily recognized, authorized signature to help the public distinguish legitimate bills from forgeries. The problem was solved with recently developed mechanical signature technology.

By the time Solomon came to the Treasury, the entire currency production operation had been brought back in-house, with all notes and bills printed and mechanically signed on a special paper manufactured at Treasury. Despite the improvement, the new operation still required many clerks to trim and cut the bills. When the Treasurer decided that the young men now performing this operation could better serve the nation at the front, muskets in their hands instead of shears, women were brought in to fill their places.

Solomon immediately saw an opportunity. A manpower shortage so serious that women had to be brought in as replacements meant that there might also be office work opportunities for men of color in jobs traditionally reserved for white men. His military service as a presidential guard would be to his benefit if he applied for one of these jobs, as there would be no questions about why he was not at the front fighting in one of the colored units.

To better understand the financial environment in which he now delivered messages, and to prepare himself for any job opportunities that might result from the ongoing shortage of white men, Solomon began "reading law," an after-work apprenticeship in which he studied law under the supervision of a lawyer. When he heard that Union Army General O. O. Howard, would soon be starting a college for colored men and women in the District, he resolved to enroll.

During the period he served with the Union Light Guard, Solomon lodged with the rest of his unit in a temporary barracks near the White House. No longer with the Guard, he now had to find new living quarters. Since he still regularly shaved the president and cut his hair and was on good terms with his former fellow guards, he was allowed keep his space at the barracks until he found new lodging.

The search was difficult as racial tensions in Washington had escalated. *The Compromise of 1850* had banned the slave trade in Washington, but as a courtesy to the South, Congress passed a stronger version of the 1793 Fugitive Slave Law. The tighter law stipulated that Northerners could be prosecuted for aiding or hiding runaway slaves. Slaveholders could go north and forcibly take custody of people they claimed to be slaves that had escaped from them. These new provisions meant that whenever a slaveholder swore that a person was his slave, federal marshals were bound to seize the alleged fugitive. Citizens could be drafted to assist in such captures, and those who refused to cooperate were liable to arrest and heavy fines. In response to this oppressive legislation, abolitionists expanded the Underground Railroad and extended it to Canada.

Because of the Compromise, Washington was no longer a depot for interstate slave trade. But traders continued their business on the other side of the Potomac in Virginia. Even though the 1850 law outlawed importing slaves into the District, Washingtonians could still own, buy and sell local slaves. Slavers worried that the Compromise might soon lead to the outlawing of slavery altogether in Washington.

In 1850, almost 27 percent of Washington's Negro population was enslaved. Although the updated Fugitive Slave Law made it more dangerous, enslaved people in the District continued to escape. By 1860, only 22 percent of the population remained enslaved. As the Civil War began in 1861, Congress passed the Confiscation Act which empowered Union forces to emancipate slaves whose owners were found to have used them to assist Confederate forces. Understandably, many were disappointed that the law also did not apply to slaves of owners in loyal slave states.

By late 1861, with the Civil War raging and most secessionist representatives gone from the Capitol, a bill had finally been introduced to Congress that would emancipate all slaves in the District. The proposed law infuriated not only slaveholders, but most white Washingtonians who still held pro-slavery leanings and supported the South. A resolution from the City's Board of Aldermen warned that the bill would have the effect of:

Converting this city ... into an asylum for free Negroes—a population undesirable in Every American community.

One alderman went further, ominously warning:

If this spirit of fanaticism will prevail, we will be in the midst of horrors we never dreamed of. It will be a question of equality or extermination. The races can never exist together as equals.

Imminent passage of the emancipation bill resulted in major black migration into Washington. Combined with the simultaneous influx of white soldiers and European immigrants, the city was stretched beyond its capacity. Most of the incoming Negroes were poor and uneducated. But because wartime demand for unskilled workers was high, many of the new arrivals found work. To the extent they were able, many black Washingtonians attempted to assist the new arrivals. Elizabeth Keckley's *Contraband Relief Association* became a major provider of relief and assistance.

In September of 1864, Solomon began his search for lodging. It was a daunting task, as wartime Washington was not the cosmopolitan urban center it would later become. Except for the more well-maintained area around the White-House complex, the District of Columbia was more like a rural town than the nation's capital. With Pennsylvania Avenue the only paved thoroughfare, many streets were often unfit for travel, dusty in the summertime, muddy in winter. The first horse-drawn street cars had recently begun to operate, running from the Navy Yard to Georgetown. The tracks of these vehicles together with those of the endless lines of quartermaster wagons deeply rutted local roads.

There were only two short sewers in the entire city, and during wet conditions, they would back up into the cellars of homes and stores along Pennsylvania Avenue. Cattle, goats, and sheep often rooted the streets, and hogs frequently wallowed in the gutters. Sidewalks were crowded with Union soldiers on patrol or leave, and many houses hid

Confederate spies and subversives who would escape across the Potomac to Virginia when cornered. To protect against Confederate invasions such as the attack on Fort Stevens in which the president was nearly killed by a sharpshooter, the city was encircled by forty-eight Union forts and eighteen hospitals.

Solomon began his lodging search in Foggy Bottom, an old neighborhood west of the White House in the District's Northwest quadrant. He had first visited the area the previous month on one of the downtown walks he frequently took on his noon meal break. Though not the most attractive of the city's residential neighborhoods, the hardscrabble area drew Solomon in because of its proximity to the Treasury building and its affordable lodging that would allow him to save toward purchasing his own home.

The neighborhood had picked up its distinctive name due to its low-lying marshy location along the Potomac River, an area that was afflicted with concentrations of fog and the smoke from nearby factories. A half-mile walk from the Treasury Building, the neighborhood's "Alley Life," consisted of squares of housing separated by open spaces inhabited by poor squatters. Unable to find affordable indoor lodging, these unfortunates lived in tents and one-or-two-room shanties. Overcrowding in the area was the result of an influx of immigrants and ex-slaves who had come to work at the nearby breweries, glass plants, and the city's gas works. Though both blacks and whites lived in Foggy Bottom, they did not live in harmony. Many of the city's new arrivals were Irish who had fled the blight that had ravaged Ireland's potato fields in the 1840s. These new arrivals often joined forces with other white American workers to force employers to hire them rather than Negroes. The resulting animosity caused frequent racial confrontations and violence.

Solomon was almost ready to abandon his search in the troubled area when he noticed a "Room for Let" sign in a modest row house on the corner of 24th and H Streets. Encouraged by a chat about neighborhood issues and challenges with Elijah Watts, the ardent abolitionist who operated the boarding house, Solomon took the small room.

Though nothing was explicitly discussed, it was his impression that the elderly proprietor might somehow be involved with the Underground Railroad.

A few days later, Solomon moved his belongings from the Union Guard barracks to his new Foggy Bottom quarters. He took to the neighborhood quickly and enjoyed frequent conversations with his landlord. He learned that his daily walks to and from the Treasury Building took him past another rowhouse on H and 22nd that had once been an important Underground Railroad stop. The blue wood-framed house had been owned by Leonard Grimes, who came to Washington in 1826 and found work with a local slaveholder. When Grimes witnessed the beating of an enslaved woman who refused to leave her dying child to go to work, he quit his job and later became the proprietor of a successful hackney coach business, one of the few occupations allowed to Negroes in DC at that time. Transporting passengers around the city area in horse-drawn taxis gave Grimes an opportunity to secretly escort enslaved people to freedom.

Things went well for Grimes until 1839 when he was spotted transporting an escaped slave and her six children out of Washington. A pro-slavery neighbor reported him to the woman's owner who swore out a warrant. Grimes was arrested, and after a trial that attracted great attention, was convicted of aiding the escape of a slave. After serving a two-year sentence, he and his family left DC and settled in Boston where he became a minister and pastor of the 12th Street Baptist Church. Because of his continued involvement and leadership in local Underground Railroad activities, his Boston church came to be known as the *Fugitive Slave Church*.

Moved by the story of the intrepid conductor and its unfortunate outcome, Solomon began reading about the history of the Underground Railroad, both locally and nationally. He was fascinated to learn of the 1848 Pearl Incident in which 77 slaves attempted an escape from the District on a stolen schooner, *The Pearl*. In the largest non-violent attempted escape in US history, the slaves were assisted by white abolitionists and members of the Grimes family. They had intended to sail north 225 miles to New Jersey, but two days into the escape, the trip was interrupted by a windstorm, the ship intercepted, and the slaves returned to their owners. Escape leaders were separated from their families and sold to slavers in the deep South.

Inspired by his reading, Solomon found himself reassessing his own situation. Although he had lived his whole life in a society defined by slavery and harsh fugitive slave laws, he had been shielded from many racial injustices because he had been born free, the son of a successful barber and prosperous landowner. In contrast to the daring of escaped slaves and Underground Railroad conductors who risked all to help them to freedom, Solomon had lived a privileged life. Although he had always been proud of his role in his earlier rescue of the missing boys in Columbus, he believed he could now do more.

<hr>

Midway through his first month at Treasury, just as he was learning all the buildings and message pickup and delivery stops on his route, Solomon was put on special assignment in the Treasury Vault area to assist in the maintenance of newly installed "burglar proof" safes that required constant maintenance and attention. The new assignment extended his workday since he still had to make his messenger rounds after he performed his vault room duties. But despite the long hours, Solomon enjoyed the assignment, as it gave him an opportunity to learn and gain experience working with new technology.

For security purposes, each worker on the vault maintenance team had responsibility for only a very small segment of the vault. Only the top officials knew the full details of the vault construction and why the massive units were designated as burglar proof. But over his weeks on the assignment, Solomon heard informal, word-of-mouth descriptions of what made the vaults so special. Apparently, the walls and doors of the huge enclosures were lined with several layers of steel plates, the space between each plate filled with cast iron balls. Word had it that the balls would move freely if in contact with a drill, thus protecting the vault from thieves and burglars. No one Solomon worked with in the Vault Department knew how well the innovative construction actually protected against break-ins. But the entire unit was so heavily guarded, it seemed highly unlikely that a burglar could get near the vaults, let alone attempt a break-in.

By the fall of 1864, Solomon knew the Treasury Department well. He was surprised and alarmed by the many government workers he encountered who expressed Confederate leanings. Even though he knew the District was very pro-South, he never expected to hear government employees speak in support of the Confederacy, especially in Treasury which had positioned itself as able to repel any rebel attacks, or in the War Department, the Union's nerve center for waging war against the confederacy.

In the War Building for his latest delivery, Solomon heard a civilian clerk, Louis Weichman, express pro-secessionist views in an animated conversation with coworkers. Solomon had come to the War Building to hand deliver a letter to army captain Daniel Gleason, Weichman's supervisor. On each of his previous deliveries, Solomon had heard Weichman expound on his pro-slavery, anti-union opinions and his resentment of Lincoln. While Weichman never seemed to mind that Solomon overheard his anti-Union rants, the talkative clerk appeared to restrain himself when the captain or any other uniformed personnel were within earshot.

As Solomon handed Captain Gleason his message, he cautiously mentioned the negative rhetoric he heard every time he was in the area. He had intended to keep his nose out of the unpleasant situation, but Weichman's latest comments were so vicious and anti-black, Solomon couldn't restrain himself. He had briefly chatted with Gleason on a previous visit and had mentioned his own military service. Because Gleason was a Northerner who seemed to appreciate Solomon's experience as the only Negro in an all-white presidential guard unit, Solomon felt it would be safe to tell him of the seditious comments he continued to hear. Gleason accepted his mail, stared at Solomon briefly, then beckoned him into his office, closed the door, and told him to take a seat.

"Yeah, I've known about Weichman's views for some time," the young officer began. "Many in the department don't like his attitude, and a few have mentioned their concerns to me. I appreciate that, just as I appreciate you speaking up."

Gleason paused for a moment, then continued. "So you're probably wondering how is it that Weichman still works in the War Department if his secessionist views are known."

The captain stood, stepped around his desk, and stopped in front of Solomon. "Believe it or not," he went on, "there's a long history of those same views within the War Department. Sadly, some of them are shared at the most senior levels. Our previous Secretary of War was a secession supporter and surrounded himself with like-minded staff, both civilian and military. When President Lincoln took over from Buchanan, most of them were immediately replaced. But many of these old mid-level managers and supervisors are still around. They aren't vocal with their anti-Union attitudes, and most are secretive about their politics. Weichman knows he's got cover among this group. Every time I've tried to get rid of him, they protect him.

"Weichman tries not to let me hear him, but whenever he has the chance, he's preaching to his coworkers. I'm guessing he's also passing information to the Confederates, but I haven't yet caught him in the act. The top brass tells me to hold my horses, as they can't get rid of all the bad apples at once. They say we must keep a few experienced people around to run things while we train replacements. So that's the situation we've got to live with, for now," Gleason added as he opened his office door and thanked Solomon for alerting him.

Usually upbeat, Solomon left the War Building in an unsettled mood. With such a treasonous but proudly held attitude, how could this Weichman still be working anywhere in the federal government, Solomon wondered. And in the War Department? It made no sense. Knowing that Lincoln walked, unaccompanied, from the White House to the War Building every evening, how could Gleason and his superior officers not see the danger of having people like Weichman in the War Building or anywhere they might cross paths with the president? How could these bureaucrats not see how easy it would be to harm or abduct the president during one of his solitary walks?

Solomon remembered how frequently Union Guard commanders had tried to dissuade the President from putting himself in harm's way with his walks, all the while knowing he didn't take their concerns seriously. But with his November reelection, the risks and stakes were higher than ever. During the presidential campaign, opponent Democratic Party strategists had introduced a new term: 'miscegenation,' mixing of the races. The pro-South public was outraged when Lincoln and his Republican allies were accused of having adopted and promoted a policy of racial intermarriage. With matters not going well for the Confederacy in the third year of the war, political tensions were further heightened.

Presented with clear, first-hand evidence of new dangers and risks, perhaps the president could finally be convinced of the need for tighter security precautions, not only for his daily walks, but for all aspects of his public and family life. Solomon resolved that he would personally make the case to his former Light Guard commander when he was in the White House a few days later to cut the president's hair.

IX

Barber Shop

...

If you can dream—and not make dreams your master;
If you can think—and not make thoughts your aim;
If you can meet with Triumph and Disaster
And treat those two impostors just the same;
If you can bear to hear the truth you've spoken
Twisted by knaves to make a trap for fools,
Or watch the things you gave your life to, broken,
And stoop and build 'em up with worn-out tools:

...

If you can talk with crowds and keep your virtue,
Or walk with Kings—nor lose the common touch,
If neither foes nor loving friends can hurt you,
If all men count with you, but none too much;
If you can fill the unforgiving minute
With sixty seconds' worth of distance run,
Yours is the Earth and everything that's in it,
And—which is more—you'll be a Man, my son!

Rudyard Kipling

Although Solomon was elated that his appointment to Treasury provided him with an opportunity to begin an exciting new career in government finance and administration, he wanted to continue his barbering work. His ongoing relationship with an esteemed client list that included the president and other high-ranking government officials had established him as a respected District barber. It had been his plan to parlay his fortuitous White House assignment into an ongoing barbering enterprise, either through private appointments or by opening a high-end shop to continue serving the president and others in Washington DC political and social circles.

But now, with his new position at Treasury, full-time proprietorship of his own shop was no longer an option. Partnering with other properly credentialled barbers, however, would allow him to lend his prestige to an existing first-class operation in which he could work limited hours to service special clients. After discussing the idea with several prospective collaborators, Solomon reached an agreement with Fred Woods, a fellow member of St. Lukes who had recently taken ownership of District of Columbia Tonsorial Services, a three-chair, high-end establishment in which Woods had served his apprenticeship and barbered for many years. Solomon would be listed as one of the shop's senior barbers and would service special customers at the end of his Treasury workday. As his schedule permitted, Solomon might occasionally join Woods during daytime business hours.

Although the attractive, well-situated shop now incorporated the latest in equipment and amenities, it continued the traditional racial structure of successful antebellum barber shops, white patrons and black barbers. Following that model, which dated back to the earliest days of the Union, Charles Thompson, the previous owner, had become wealthy and had started many new barbers on successful careers of their own.

Born a slave in early 1800s Ohio, Thompson learned as a young man how slave barbers leveraged close ties to their masters and a familiarity with their culture into opportunities to gain their freedom and own barbershops. He had also been taught barbering by his father who, for many years, had worked as a "waiting man" for a wealthy Ohio planter, a prestigious position for a slave of the era. In that capacity, Charles's father had served his master variously as a valet, barber, messenger, and at times an overseer of other slaves.

The opportunity for slaves to learn such important skills as barbering, caring for and styling wigs, and even rendering basic medical services, resulted from the reluctance of many white men—particularly those who had recently arrived from Europe—to perform personal services. Even though colored men of the antebellum period, both free and enslaved, were systematically barred from most skilled trades, they flourished as barbers. The first-class barber shop business model they developed provided comfortable destinations where white patrons could enjoy each other's company as they received their haircuts and shaves. Establishing relationships with influential whites in this manner, black barbers like Thompson were able to accumulate wealth, buy their freedom, and establish their own businesses.

Despite the prestige and earning power of barbering, the path to success was not always welcoming, as colored barbers were sometimes treated with contempt and disrespect. Strangely, the master's posture toward the trusted aide who regularly held a razor to his neck was, at best, one of patronizing tolerance. To maintain their sanity and sustain their businesses, black barbers had to anesthetize themselves to the toxic atmosphere associated with providing first class services to often-unappreciative clients. Although Thompson's demeanor toward his almost exclusively white customer base had to be simultaneously conservative and cheerfully subservient, he reconciled this difficult-to-maintain public face with the knowledge that he was not only providing a good life for his family but was also helping to build a strong and enduring component of black economic prosperity.

Much like Thompson in demeanor, convictions and politics, Solomon was conservative in his attitudes about race relations. He did not expect to see racial integration in the near future, and in business matters, he advocated separatism and self-help. Although he believed that people of color should fight relentlessly for full freedom and equal rights, he was convinced that a barber shop could not be successful unless it served whites only. He made it clear to Woods that his involvement in the shop would require that such a policy be maintained. With the substantial book of business that Solomon could bring to the shop, he knew that woods would accede to his wishes.

Solomon did not believe his conservative business attitudes conflicted with his commitment to freedom from social and political restrictions. He rationalized that segregation imposed equal restrictions on all races and that both whites and blacks had to be mindful of their boundaries. To him, what mattered more than integration was the need for businessmen of color to build wealth, provide training and business opportunities to other Negroes, and contribute to the collective wealth and economic stability of the black community.

In the spring of 1864, new space for the shop was secured on the first floor of a new three-story office building on Fifteenth Street NW, midway between St. Lukes and the White House. New chairs were ordered, and work commenced to prepare the facility for a late Spring opening. Solomon assisted Woods in the screening and interviewing of barbers. Announcements were posted in the Treasury, War Department, and Navy Department Buildings and mailed to the White House and Congressional Offices. Solomon used his network of White House and Department level contacts to spread the word and secure early appointments.

As preparations for opening proceeded, Woods asked Solomon to reconsider his position on strict customer segregation. He told Solomon about the enthusiastic celebration of emancipation among colored barbers in Boston and how some of the more radical among them had decided to not only begin servicing black customers, but to no longer accommodate whites. When Woods was unable to respond to Solomon's question about the business impact of such bold policies, Solomon opined that there would be devasting bottom-line losses for any barber shop that discouraged white patronage in any way. While he acknowledged that there was an unmet need for barbering services among potential black customers, he strongly believed that any income possible from such sources could, in no way, compensate for the corresponding losses of white customer revenues. Whatever revenue that could come from providing the basic haircuts that Negroes had long received at home could not make up for the enormous losses that would accrue when elaborate hair cutting, styling, dyeing or wig making services were no longer provided to affluent white customers. And there was no middle ground, Solomon insisted. White customers would no longer accept service from a colored barber if they suspected that his tools had been used on Negro hair, even if the services had been rendered in a private off-site appointment.

When Fred countered that it was the responsibility of all Negro businessmen to support non-financial elements of emancipation such as freedom from discrimination and segregation, Solomon responded that economic strength was the most important, if not the only true measure of individual liberty and dignity. "If you're broke, you have no dignity," Solomon added. "And if you have financial strength, you can buy all the dignity you need."

"With all due respect, I couldn't disagree more," Fred answered. "For way too long, we've struggled under the thumb of the white man. It matters little whether we are free or still enslaved, or what kind of a fortune we may have amassed; one snap of a white man's fingers can end our freedoms and our lives. Those days should be over."

Fred continued. "One other thing. If the top black barbers in the District continue to serve white patrons only, must colored men continue to seek bootleg, amateur haircuts on their porches or backyards? Where do you get your hair cut?" Fred queried Solomon.

"I agree with you that the self-pride and sense of equality that should follow emancipation is important, if not essential, to our survival," Solomon shot back. "But what does that self-pride mean if we still have to beg the white man for handouts and menial jobs? Sure, it would be nice if we could all be prideful, outspoken warrior leaders like Harriet Tubman or Frederick Douglass. But the reality is that most of us will have to fight quietly from the trenches, doing the dirty work, adhering to onerous rules, and taking the often-unpleasant steps necessary to accumulate the means to be the white man's equal and get him off our back.

"As to the decision of some Boston black barbers to no longer serve white customers, that is pretty much an invitation for a new class of white barbers to fill the gap in what has heretofore been a lucrative all-colored profession. Seems like the makings of a self-inflicted wound to me.

And as to my own hair," he added, "since I've been in Washington, I've regularly exchanged haircuts with a good barber friend of mine who lives in Alexandria. We alternate our sessions between each other's homes. It would be preferable not to have to go to such lengths to get a haircut. But I just take it as a cost of doing business. I try to think of it as an opportunity to spend an evening with a dear friend."

Although Solomon and Fred would never see eye to eye on the optimum long-term strategy for full emancipation, they agreed, at least initially, to adhere to whites-only customer restrictions. On August 10, 1864, the shop reopened its doors to an all-white customer contingent.

By lunchtime on opening day, the shop was crowded with first-time and returning customers on hand to see the facility and enjoy complementary refreshments. Fred had brought in another barber, and two chairs were busy throughout most of the morning. Several appointment-request messages had also been received. Enjoying the men's club atmosphere while waiting to be serviced, many of the mostly government-worker patrons reveled in visiting with each other and discussing news and events of the day. When several Treasury Department workers and White House staffers stopped in at the end of their workday, a lively discussion about the future of the Confederacy began as they waited their turns for shaves and haircuts.

Interoffice competition between the two governmental units drew other patrons into the animated discussion. Although both groups were part of the same Republican administration, the Treasury people worked for and supported the views of Treasury Secretary Salmon

Chase, a radical who believed that citizens of Confederate states who had supported the Confederacy should lose their right to vote, and that lawyers and teachers among that group should not be allowed to continue their professions. Chase's supporters further believed that slavery should be abolished without compensation to slaveholders and that new freedmen should have the vote.

The White House group supported the more conservative views of Lincoln, who preferred compensated emancipation and a less punitive position on voting rights of citizens in Confederate states. "With malice toward none with charity for all" as expressed in his second inaugural address, the president favored returning the vote to all those who would take an oath to uphold the Union and emancipation.

The intensity of the impromptu debate increased when one of Lincoln's men criticized the unseemliness of Chase's anticipated competition with Lincoln, his boss, for the 1864 Republican presidential nomination. Solomon was in the shop during the debate but declined to weigh in and take a debate position. He was happy to see a robust discussion that seemed to heighten the convivial barbershop atmosphere he and Fred had sought to create. He looked forward to many more such occurrences.

⊷◦⊷

Troubled that he and Fred Woods disagreed on the shop's white's only customer policy, Solomon sought the advice of his father. Shortly after the reopening of the refurbished shop, he wrote his father, telling him of his concerns and asking for his input. He also invited him to come to the District and visit the shop. In his letter, he confided that in recent months he had quietly begun to question his customer service restrictions, which he had to acknowledge were racist. It had begun to trouble him that these policies were not consistent with full emancipation. He confided that he now felt some shame that he continued to reject the righteous desire, shared by many young barbers, to pursue the true spirit of emancipation by serving black customers.

Two weeks later, Hanson was in Washington for a long weekend. He had long looked forward to the visit as he had not been in the city since the end of Solomon's Union guard service and the beginning of his Treasury job. Solomon brought an extra bed into his Foggy Bottom quarters for the occasion. On Thursday, July 14, after a tour of the Treasury Building, he escorted his father into the refurbished District of Columbia Tonsorial Services where Fred Woods and a second barber cut hair, and several customers chatted as they waited to be serviced. After introductions to Fred and his assistant, Solomon and Hanson took seats in the waiting area and observed the shop's operation. An hour later, they left the shop and walked two blocks to a nearby eatery where they sat down for lunch.

"I like the layout of the shop," Hanson began, "and Fred looks like a good fellow to work with." After small talk about equipment and chair arrangement, Hanson turned to the customer race problem Solomon had written to him about.

"I've thought a lot about your issue," Hanson continued, "and it's a tough one. No question that if you try to serve colored and white customers together, you will cut into your high-end service revenues. No doubt about it. In Columbus, most of our customers, by far, have always been white. As you know, we've always been able to sidestep the issue by scheduling our few colored customers so that the races never mix or even see each other. And since we work out of our home by appointment, customers don't know anything about other customers they can't see.

Now, I suppose if we start servicing more colored customers, the chances will increase that the whites will figure out what is going on. But that hasn't happened yet."

"You're in a different situation," Hanson added, as he enjoyed the final forkful of his baked chicken and candied sweet potatoes. "Since your facility is open to the public, your customer mix is highly visible. If you begin servicing any black customers, white customers will know quickly and react.

"But times are changing. We can't fight for change and at the same time cling to the part of an ugly past that fills our pocketbook. And not every white customer will refuse to be around colored ones. Especially in this city. I'm sure there are plenty of abolitionists and radical Republicans who will be just fine around colored customers. Hell, if you begin serving both races openly, you might very well become one of the preferred spots for the more progressive crowd."

"I can't argue with that," Solomon responded. "I'm not yet sure how we're going to do it, but I guess we'll have to figure out a way to soften our 'whites only' customer policy. But by doing so, we'll have to prepare to lose a good segment of our white customers. And we'll likely be opening the door for a whole new class of white barbers in what has heretofore been a lucrative all-black profession in the District." Solomon sighed. "I know it's important to keep up with the times, but like the old folks always say, 'progress never comes without pain.'"

X

Secret Societies

You can't separate peace from freedom because no one can be at peace unless he has his freedom.

Malcolm X

The Knights of the Golden Circle (KGC) was not the only organization attempting to shape the social and political climate of a nation at war with itself. Others advocating for change included the predominantly white Scottish Rite Freemasons who had practiced their craft in America since the early eighteenth century, and the all-black Prince Hall Freemasons who had established their first US lodge in 1792. The terrorist Ku Klux Klan, which emerged as the Civil War ended, was successor to the equally violent and subversive KGC.

Although nominally distinct, some structural elements of all these societies were similar. In all but one of them there was synergy and often collaboration. But only in the group shunned by all the others, the Prince Hall Freemasons, could Solomon or any other black man in America hope to become a member.

In colonial days, white Masonic leaders in the US modelled their lodges as political associations similar to lodges they had visited in the British Empire prior to the Revolutionary War. These Scottish Rite lodges accepted slavery and did not welcome black members. Following uprisings in Mexico and the Caribbean, such as the slave revolt of the 1790s, that created Haiti as an independent republic, many embittered slave owners sought common cause in Masonry and established Scottish Rite lodges in the South. Many hoped to continue their slave plantations in territories occupied by the US after the 1846 Mexican War.

Black Masonry was established in the US by ex-slave Prince Hall, an abolitionist leader in the free colored community of Boston. When his petition for admittance to the all-white St. Johns Lodge of Boston was denied, Hall sought admission into the Grand Lodge of Ireland and was initiated in 1775. Returning to the US, he formed the African Grand Lodge of North America and served as its Grand Master until his death in 1807. In subsequent years, black Masonry spread throughout the US as Negroes continued to be barred from most Scottish Rite lodges. In June, 1847, black Masons came together for a National Compact to establish a nationwide governance structure. The resulting coalition became known as the Prince Hall Affiliation Masons. Hanson Johnson, a prominent Ohio Mason, was a key organizer of the Boston meeting.

Solomon harbored mixed feelings about Masonry. He had always admired Prince Hall lodges for bringing men of color together, not only to support each other as brothers, but to set an example of righteous behavior for the larger society. He was particularly proud of black Masons for using their collective influence to improve the lives of all Americans of color, both enslaved and free. He respected his father's long Masonic service and his important role in establishing the African Grand Lodge. Most of all he appreciated how his father had often provided cover and shelter to escaping slaves by using his Columbus rental properties as Underground Railroad Way Stations whenever they were not occupied by tenants. But it had always troubled Solomon that such an important component of Negro life in America as Prince Hall Masonry began as the unwanted offspring of a racist group that did not accept black members. To him, it was an embarrassment that, in order to start their own lodge, Negroes had to first ask for permission from the very same men who would never accept them as either brothers or equals. Even worse, US Scottish Rite lodges labelled Prince Hall Lodges as "clandestine."

In the runup to the Civil War, growth in Prince Hall Masonry had been spurred by disturbing trends in US slaveholder policies that were not always visible to the general public but were usually supported by white Masonic leaders. As early as the Mexican War, slaveholders pushed for the annexation of Mexico and the liberation of Cuba from Spanish rule so that both could become US slave states. In 1850, such a plan was promoted by slave-holding Mississippi Governor John Quitman, a former US Army general who had been appointed military governor of Mexico City at the end of the Mexican war. Quitman was the Sovereign Inspector General of the Scottish Rite of Freemasonry in the South and a leader in the secessionist movement.

When his annexation effort failed, Quitman was indicted by a federal grand jury for violating US neutrality laws and was forced to resign from the post of governor to defend himself. After a federal trial produced a hung jury, Quitman revived his plans for the Cuba invasion. Encouraged by President Franklin Pierce, Quitman organized a private army of more than 15,000 mercenaries by amalgamating the secessionist Knights of the Golden Circle with other Southern rights organizations such as The Order of the Lone Star of the West. But Quitman was forced to abort the mission when Pierce suddenly reversed his earlier approval of the invasion.

When Quitman died unexpectedly, his Masonic fellow Mexican War veteran and staunch pro-slavery advocate, Albert Pike, was elevated to the position of Sovereign Grand Commander of the Scottish Rite for the Southern Jurisdiction. As such, he took over Quitman's position as the top-ranking Freemason in the US. Like Quitman before him, Pike's actions did not reflect positively on Freemasonry. As a Confederate Army General, he had commanded a unit that was accused of war crimes such as scalping Union Army prisoners. A man of many faces, Pike wrote and spoke publicly of Masonic integrity and uprighteousness. But to him, Masonic principles and brotherly love applied only to white men. As a high-ranking official of the Ku Klux Klan, he was deeply opposed to Negro suffrage.

From his position as Masonic Sovereign Grand Commander, Pike expounded on the high ideals and principles of Freemasonry. To a large St. Louis audience, he once said:

> God pity the man who will not lay on the altar of Masonry, every feeling of ill-will in his heart to a brother Mason. Freemasonry is one faith, one great religion, one great common altar, around which all men, of all tongues and all languages can assemble. And Masonry will never be true to her mission till we all join hands, heart to heart and hand to hand, around the altar of Masonry, with a determination that Masonry shall become at some time worthy of her pretensions—no longer a pretender to that which is good: but that she shall be an apostle of peace, good will, charity, and toleration.

But, flushed with racial privilege and smug superiority, Pike often expressed less lofty views. In a letter to his brother about recognition of black Masonry, he opined:

> Our people only stave off the question by saying that Negro Masons here are clandestine.

> I think there is no middle ground between rigid exclusion of Negroes or recognition and affiliation with the whole mass.

> I am not inclined to meddle in the matter. I took my obligation to white men not Negroes. When I have to accept Negroes as brothers or leave Masonry, I shall leave it.

> I am interested to keep the Ancient and Accepted Rite uncontaminated, in our country, at least, by the leprosy of Negro Association.

By 1827, the African Grand Lodge had declared independence from the United Grand Lodge of England, just as the white Grand Lodge of Massachusetts had done in 1782. The new African Grand Lodge also separated itself from all white grand lodges in the US and declared itself an independent Masonic body. This led to chartering of colored lodges throughout North America.

Solomon had never understood why black Masons worked so hard for entry into an organization that wanted no part of them. Rather than go to Europe and beg for crumbs from the table of Scottish Rite Masons, he believed colored men could have set a better example of dignity and self-determination by creating their own independent fraternal organization that had no ties to, and used none of the secrets, symbols, or rituals of Scottish Rite Masonry. Out of respect for his father, Solomon never spoke of these views. But having reached manhood without taking steps toward Prince Hall membership, it was obvious that he had reservations and concerns about Masonry.

His attitude began to change on September 19, 1864, the fateful Thursday afternoon that runaway slaves Eliza Cobbins and her daughter Cleo burst into Mount Zion AME Church as he and several other prospective members were being introduced to the church's Men's Guild. A distraught and panting Eliza told the group that she and her daughter had accompanied their mistress on a trip from her Maryland farm to a family gathering in Washington. She and Cleo fled two hours earlier when she was informed that Cleo had been sold to a Mississippi family that would arrive later that same evening to claim her. Under the ruse that she and Cleo were going to their temporary basement quarters to pack Cleo's few belongings, the two quietly slipped out of a window and disappeared into a nearby alley. Not knowing where to find safety, they stumbled into Foggy Bottom. When they thought they saw pursuers, they ran into the nearest shelter, the small Mt. Zion church build-ing on the corner of 27th and P Streets NW.

A few Guild members were sympathetic to the predicament of the two unexpected visitors, but most worried that, according to Fugitive Slave Law, the Guild could be charged with aiding and abetting an es-cape if slavecatchers discovered Eliza and Cleo at the church. Surprised that there could be such fears in a church founded only a few years ear-lier by ex-slaves, many of whom were runaways, Solomon volunteered to escort the two escapees to his boarding house for temporary shelter. He took the chance that his abolitionist landlord might be able to help with escape planning.

With Eliza and Cleo disguised in baggy work shirts and wide-brimmed floppy hats, Solomon and fellow Guild members Amos Jack-son and Carl Watson left the church and guided the two escapees to Foggy Bottom. An hour later, after eleven blocks of anxious walking and avoiding crowds, the party arrived safely at the small hostelry. Mr. Watts and his wife graciously received the two nervous runaways and tried to calm them with assurances that things would work out well. When Solomon asked about the horse-drawn wagon hitched in front of the house, Watts told him that a neighborhood hackney named Robert Jenkins was unloading trunks for a new resident.

"Do you think he might be willing to hire out with his wagon for a few hours to get Ms. Eliza and her daughter safely out of the District?" Solomon asked.

"Possibly so," Watts responded. "He helped me move passengers many times before Lincoln ended slavery here in the District. Back then, it was usually men trying to get to the Anacostia River dock. Their cover was that they were merchant seamen looking for their next job. These guys usually traveled alone so that they could move quickly and not expose their families to capture or injury. Usually, their plan was to find work, save money, and purchase their wives and children through a third party. In the few cases Robert transported a woman, she'd been with a man.

"Later, after Lincoln's proclamation and the abolition of slavery in the Confederacy, Underground Railroad activities pretty much ended. But with continuing escapes from Northern states where slavery hasn't yet been abolished, from time to time there is still a need to move runaways secretly in order to avoid Fugitive Slave Law recaptures."

Watts continued, smiling gently at Cleo and her mother. "So, I've got an idea. Although Robert's work usually involves moving furniture and trunks around town, occasionally he transports people sitting on benches in the covered portion of a large two-horse buggy he owns with his two brothers. He keeps a piece of black tarpaulin in the rig. Sometimes he hangs it in the rear of the wagon, allowing a foot or two behind it to hide his belongings. If the wagon is temporarily unattended, and someone peeks through the opening behind the driver's seat into the back of the wagon looking for something to steal, they see nothing, as the tarp appears to be the back of the wagon.

"Since seeking work at the dock is not a good cover story for these two young ladies, perhaps Robert will be willing to hide them behind the tarp in his wagon and carry them north over the Maryland border to Silver Spring. It's only six miles to the border, and we've got contacts in Silver Spring. Even though Maryland is still a slave state, our people could provide them cover on their first stop toward Canada.

Before another word was spoken, Eliza jumped to her feet. With tears streaming down her face, she took Cleo's hand and moved toward the door.

"Where are you going child?" Mrs. Watts asked. "You can't go outside by yourself right now. There is likely a search party already looking for you. I've got supper almost ready. Don't drag this baby out into the street on an empty stomach."

"But I've got no money to pay for all of this! Not a single cent!" cried the frustrated young mother. "I appreciate what you folks are trying to do for me and Cleo, but it just won't work."

"Why don't we just calm down a moment?" Solomon asked as he stepped between Eliza and the door. "You're on the first step of an important journey. Let's not get bogged down with concerns about money. The costs will be covered. I'll make that commitment."

"I'll share them with you, Solomon." Amos blurted out before Eliza had a chance to respond.

"Cut me in for a portion of them, as well," added Carl Watson, ending the discussion.

"Now all we have to do is to convince Robert to take on the mission. He should be back any minute from an errand to the feed store," Watts added, the tension dissipating as everyone sat down to enjoy the meal Mrs. Watts had prepared.

Upon his return, Robert agreed to conduct the trip and drop his passengers off at the home of Jason Dickie, a farmer in Sligo, a small town just across the Maryland border near Silver Spring. He suggested they leave as soon as possible as the rainfall that had just begun would make for lighter traffic and would likely discourage search parties. He wanted to take advantage of the few hours of remaining daylight so as not to have to travel in the dark. At sunset, gaslights would be lit along the downtown portion of the 16th Street route on which he planned to travel north. But only the first mile or so of the street had lighting. Beyond that point, 16th became a dark and foreboding country road. Robert didn't want to risk a wagon breakdown or an interception on an isolated dirt road. Fugitive Slave laws meant that runaways could be recovered at any time and in any location.

Concerned that Robert might need help avoiding or confronting search parties in the District and points north, Solomon volunteered to accompany the party on this first and most dangerous leg of the escape. Amos and Carl followed suit. It was decided that after Eliza and Cleo were dropped off, the rest of the escape party would sleep in the Dickie farm barn and return to the District the following morning. Solomon and his fellow Guild members had only a few coins in their pockets, but Robert agreed to be reimbursed for his costs the following week.

Watts mapped out a trip that would take Eliza and Cleo north from Silver Spring through Philadelphia, New York City, Albany, Rochester, and then to Canada. He drafted letters to conductors he knew along the way. These conductors were usually members of local Vigilance Committees that would provide shelter and money to the fugitives. Solomon was surprised and encouraged to see that the conductor named for the city of Rochester was Frederick Douglass. With people like Douglass involved, he was convinced that Eliza and Cleo would safely reach the promised land.

As Eliza folded the documents and put them in her small knapsack, Mrs. Watts pressed two dollars into her hand. When Eliza once again teared up, Mrs. Watts took the young mother and daughter in her arms.

"This will not be easy," the elderly innkeeper said gently. "Freedom is an important goal, especially when it is the only way you can protect your child. But even with trusted conductors like Robert, there will be great risks in attempting to reach Canada. Slave catchers are everywhere, and these days, they are more desperate than ever. Are you ready to take the risks?"

"Thank you for the warning, ma'am," Eliza began after pausing to collect herself. "But I don't care what the risks are. I've got to get my baby away from here. This white man who wants to take her away probably has many slaves already at his plantation. But when men like him see a pretty young girl like Cleo who has just the right color and looks, he'll want to take her home, make her a house slave, and as soon as she is in her womanly ways, use her for his pleasure. But with Cleo being only six years old, and him already an old man, he might not want to wait until she's grown before he starts his mess."

Her tearfulness changing to anger, Eliza continued: "I know what I'm talking about. It happened to my mother and also to me! I ain't going to have my baby to facing the same kind of a life!

So, with all due respect, ma'am, I could never allow some musty, wrinkled-up old slaver to use my baby for a plaything just because he's got no more feeling for the wife who gave him the one thing he wanted most: sons to carry on the family name. I couldn't live with the thought that one of these monsters would trap my baby into a living hell."

"I understand, honey," Mrs. Watts responded, still holding Eliza and Cleo close to her. "You two look like you have what it takes to make it all the way to freedom. We'll be praying for you every day and looking forward to getting the message that you've arrived safely."

Promising to write often, a tearful Eliza and Cleo set out with their travel party on the first leg of its journey to freedom. As they left, Watts wished them Godspeed. He congratulated Robert, Solomon, Amos, and Carl on their valor and expressed his appreciation for the way they responded to a crisis with no advance planning. He asked that upon their return, they join him on his porch to toast this important step toward freedom with a glass of whiskey. He expressed his hope that they could all work together again to continue the good fight.

At four p.m., with rain continuing to fall, Robert pulled his wagon onto H Street. With the two young runaways hidden safely at the rear of the wagon, and Robert, Solomon, and his two companions seated on benches at the front, the party headed east toward 16th Street where they would turn north toward the Maryland border. Situated in the middle of the wagon between the men seated at the front and the passengers hidden in the rear, there sat a trunk of men's clothing, a chest of drawers, and two duffel bags. If slavecatchers stopped them along the way, Robert would claim that he was moving Solomon and his companions to Silver Spring to begin work as field hands. If everything went as planned, they would reach the Dickie farm around six that afternoon.

As the wagon moved out of Foggy Bottom, Solomon asked Robert what motivated him to conduct slave escapes that could backfire with such serious consequences.

With a quizzical glance at Solomon, Robert haltingly replied:

"I never thought I'd ever be involved in anything like this. But a few years ago, when I lived in Boston, I became a member of a Prince Hall Lodge that was involved in Underground Railroad passages. The lodge had become a very active stop and, in some cases, temporarily hid escapees in the lodge hall until the next leg of an escape could be arranged. It wasn't long before the master of the lodge asked me to assist in an escape in which one of the conductors had taken ill at the last minute and wasn't able to participate. When the mission went well, I was asked to participate in additional escapes, and later, to lead them. That continued throughout my time in Boston. Though it had never been in my plans, I got great satisfaction helping conduct all those people to freedom."

"So why did you stop?" Solomon asked. "Did you leave Masonry?"

"No, I never left the craft," Robert answered. "I was born and raised in Washington and had moved to Boston for a position as a carpenter's apprentice. My father passed as I was completing my apprenticeship, and I moved back to the District to take care of my mother who was now alone."

"When I returned in 1862, I found work, but there were no Prince Hall lodges in the area. I've been talking to a few friends in the District about forming a lodge. One of them is from a Prince Hall lodge in Pennsylvania, but we haven't moved forward on anything yet.

"I came to know Elijah Watts through my job," Robert continued. "When I found out about the help he was providing here in the District, I felt the need to work with him. I'm still hopeful that we can form a lodge here sometime soon and build on what I've been doing with Elijah."

"I hope that comes to pass," Amos responded, with Solomon and Carl nodding in agreement. "We would like to be a part of it."

———◦◦———

Just over an hour after the Foggy Bottom departure, Robert pulled his wagon to a stop in front of the Dickie farmhouse on the outskirts of Sligo. The party was warmly welcomed by Jason Dickie and his family. Travelling in the rain had been uncomfortable, with many nervous moments as there was constant risk that the wagon might become mired in a muddy road segment. But the inclement conditions had also helped the trip to be completed safely without interference from any search parties.

Much later that night, after enjoying a snack prepared by Mrs. Dickie and retiring to the bedroll he had spread out on a pallet of hay in the Dickie barn, Solomon reflected on the unexpected events of the day and his new Masonic connection. He suddenly regretted not having joined his father's lodge. How was it, he wondered, could he have become so interested in Masonry through a chance meeting with a man he had not even known twenty-four hours earlier, when he had never responded to earlier invitations from his own father, a prominent Mason, a man of great integrity, and someone he deeply respected. With the important slave liberation that Negro Masons were supporting with their Underground Railroad service, he regretted that he had allowed himself to be disdainful of them because of the disrespect they endured from white Masons.

Things suddenly seemed clearer to him. Black Masons like his father and Prince Hall knew that America had failed to truly achieve the goals of freedom and equality described in its own Declaration of Independence. Just as these men remained in a flawed US to fight for their rights, they also recognized that Scottish Rite Masonry had failed to reach its lofty goals. They now were engaged in the struggle to bring Masonic goals to fruition for colored men. When it became clear that this could not be achieved within existing Masonic structures, they cut off all ties to US Masonry and created the African Grand Lodge.

Solomon's sudden awareness was accompanied by regret that he had not earlier had this clarity. Even though he had helped his father with Underground Railroad activities in Columbus, the two had thus far missed out on opportunities to share the bond of Masonry. But it was not too late. He resolved that, as soon as possible, he would thank his father for the outstanding example he had always set as both a man and a Mason and ask his blessings to become a fellow member of the craft.

The message was too important to be transmitted in a letter. These thoughts and feelings would have to be communicated man to man while there was still an opportunity to do so. He would have to get home very soon.

XI

Freedom Coffles

*Slavery wus a bad thing en' freedom, of de kin' we
got wid nothin' to live on wus bad.*

*Two snakes full of pisen. One lying wid his head
pintin' north, de other wid his head pintin' south.*

*Dere names wus slavery an' freedom. De snake
called slavery lay wid his head pinted south and de
snake called freedom lay wid his head pinted north.*

Both bit de nigger, an' dey wus both bad.

Patsy Mitchner

I n the fall of 1864, just weeks after he helped shepherd Eliza and Cleo to safety, Solomon met Anne Sprigg, a new clerk at the Treasury Department. Solomon welcomed her arrival, as it meant he was no longer the only person of color in Treasury's sea of whiteness. Much older than most starting clerks, Sprigg had spent many years in the Washington DC hospitality business before President Lincoln recommended for her Treasury position.

When Solomon cut the president's hair the following week and mentioned that he had met Ms. Sprigg, Lincoln told him of his fondness for the former hotelier who he had first met in 1842 when he stayed at her boarding house as a young congressman. The president remembered that Sprigg's establishment was often referred to as Abolition House because of the many abolitionist lobbyists and radical anti-slavery congressmen who boarded there.

Lincoln had pleasant memories of his stays with Ms. Sprigg, as guesthouses like hers were essential for congressmen who had to be in DC for seasonal sessions of Congress but could not yet afford to buy homes in the area or stay at expensive hotels on Pennsylvania Avenue. Although Lincoln resided at her facility for only his single term in the House of Representatives, he recalled that many congressmen stayed for years. Living with like-minded colleagues, working, and eating meals together caused residents to think of the boarding-house relationship almost as a fraternity.

The president described how, during his two-year stay, the hotel also became known as a location of odd disappearances: vanishings and departures that often involved escaped slaves that had sought cover there or bondsmen who had been hired out by their owners to work at the establishment. Lincoln explained that he was never quite sure whether Sprigg herself was involved in the disappearances, but he was certain that some of her boarders had assisted in the escapes. He believed that the guesthouse was an Underground Railroad station.

By the time Solomon met Sprigg, her boardinghouse was no longer in business. As a friendship developed between the two, she told him of her decision to close the establishment in 1861, at the beginning of the Civil War. Her husband had passed away, and as she approached sixty, she no longer had the stamina to meet the stringent demands of running a hotel, especially amidst the tumult and uncertainty in the capital of a nation preparing for war. The deciding factor, she explained, was the kidnapping of one of her servers, Henry, an enslaved man hired out to work in her dining room, and his free wife, Sylvia, a maid at the house. Slave traders broke into the hotel, seized Henry, and dragged him off to a local slave pen. Henry had raised $290 of the $350 he had agreed to pay his owner for his freedom when she sold him to the slave traders. With the help of several of her abolitionist-leaning boarders such as Congressman Joshua Giddings, Sprigg was able to purchase Henry's freedom.

Sprigg's many years as a Washington hotelier had resulted in good relations with others in the business. She convinced one of them, the proprietor of the nearby Merrick Roadhouse, to expand his business by hiring her staff and absorbing as many of her boarders and dining guests as possible. The transfer worked out well, with most of her boarders and workers moving to Merrick. With so many familiar faces on board, Merrick took on much of the Sprigg atmosphere and even inherited the informal Abolition House alias.

When Sprigg informed Solomon that the very congenial Merrick dining facility was open to the public and suggested he visit, Solomon began taking meals there. In time, he became familiar with its informal infrastructure and met many people involved in the remaining elements of the Underground Railroad. Although most Railroad lines were no longer active after the Emancipation Proclamation freed slaves in Confederate states, a few escape routes were still needed as some Southern slaveholders ignored Union rulings and kept their slaves. The secrecy of the of these remaining routes would still be crucial if future runaways were to have any hope of reaching safe havens in the North.

⋯◦⋯

Through his work with Elijah Watts, Solomon had come to believe that successful escapes always involved very small parties, most often male slaves owned by the same master. Fearing betrayal by other slaves seeking favor with the master, these cautious passengers avoided discussing their escape plans with anyone. More often than not, they travelled without their wives, children, or other family members. Reluctant to subject their families to the dangers of capture by search parties and the deprivation of traveling under cover, they preferred to journey alone and later arrange for the purchase of their loved ones through third parties.

In contrast, Abolition House missions were huge, usually involving more than a dozen runaways from Maryland or Delaware, two of the four still-enslaved border states. While trip planners and conductors were aware that smaller escape parties allowed for better concealment, they no longer had to fear interception by sheriffs and marshals in Northern states. But knowing they were still exposed to tracking and capture by slavecatchers operating under Fugitive Slave laws, conductors opted for larger parties that, if necessary, could confront and fight off pursuers.

Bondsmen from neighboring slave states who worked at Merrick Roadhouse and other nearby establishments were usually aware of upcoming escape opportunities. Despite the risks of betrayal, they informed other slaves and family members of upcoming missions whenever they returned to the master's home to turn over their earnings. Because of this information pipeline, slaves were usually aware of and eager to participate in new escape opportunities. Knowing who was ready and able to join escape missions, Abolition House conductors created trip rosters with passenger compositions that were most likely to succeed. Its most recent operation transported fifteen passengers to safety and word had it that some twenty would be liberated in the next mission.

Troubled that he had never received word from Eliza that she and her daughter had reached the Promised Land, Solomon was eager to assist in missions that moved the most people and had the highest likelihood of success. Because his Treasury job duties allowed him only limited time off, he intended to participate in only the first leg of escapes, the movement of travelers from the District to interim destinations in Maryland or Pennsylvania.

The first week in December, as he waited in the Merrick dining room for his beef stew and dumplings lunch special, Solomon was visited by a busboy carrying a tray of dirty dishes to the kitchen. The twenty-year-old bondsman glanced cautiously around the room, and in a low breath, whispered to Solomon: "The wheels will soon be turning." Making sure he was not overheard, he told Solomon that a meeting was to be held the following Wednesday so that agents could line up cargo and lay out plans for a new trip north. A day later, Frederick Inniss, Assistant Pastor of nearby St. Mary's Episcopal Church, sent a message to Solomon inviting him to attend the meeting. Having occasionally lunched and talked politics with him, Inniss knew of Solomon's willingness to assist in a transport.

Six days later, Solomon trudged through a heavy snowstorm to join the reverend, five prospective travelers, and three conductors at Merrick's. As dinner service had concluded, the group had the large dining room to itself.

Standing to face the small audience seated at two adjacent tables, Inniss began: "First, let me welcome you all to Abolition House. I know this is a serious group because following the North Star is serious business, and only the serious would come out in the storm we have tonight!

"This evening we will discuss a mission to move nineteen souls from captivity in Maryland to the Promised Land. It would be nice if all nineteen could have been here for this important meeting. But, of course, the very oppression which makes that impossible is the evil from which we hope to liberate our travelers.

"At tonight's meeting," Inniss continued, "we have in attendance five of the nineteen prospective passengers and three of the four conductors who will guide them to safety. As you probably guessed, all conductors are freedmen. But the passengers, of course, are not. Ownership of the nineteen souls is divided among three Maryland farmers. Obviously, only the five of you who have been hired out to work in the District could be with us tonight. In strict confidence, we will provide you with the names and owners of all others who will be passengers on the proposed trip. It will be your responsibility to faithfully, thoroughly, and discreetly communicate the plans discussed here tonight to those fellow travelers. It is your solemn duty to do so and maintain absolute secrecy."

Sensing tension in the group, the gregarious Inniss stepped closer to the two tables. In his most comforting pastoral tones, he attempted to reassure his small audience: "Although this is a transportation planning gathering and not a church meeting, we all understand that the plans we lay out tonight can only be accomplished with the help of God. In asking His blessing, let me quote the words of the great Harriet Tubman who, after her own escape, returned to the South nineteen times to deliver more than three hundred souls to safety. Because of her boldness, slave owners offered a forty-thousand-dollar reward for her capture, dead or alive. I had the honor of hearing her speak the following words to describe her motivation:

> I had reasoned this out in my mind; there was one of two things I had a right to, liberty or death if I could not have one, I would have the other.

"After her many years of conducting," Inniss continued, "I heard her sum up her work with these words of extraordinary humility:

> T'wasn't me, 'twas de Lord! I was conductor of the Underground Railroad for eight years, and I can say what most conductors can't say; I never run my train off the track, and I never lost a passenger.

Following "Amen" murmurs from his small audience, Inniss described the plan to move the nineteen freedom seekers on the first and most dangerous leg of a three-part liberation journey to Canada.

The first segment would begin in DC and end three days and 109 miles later in Columbia, Pennsylvania. This most perilous component would involve travel through Maryland, the only slave state on their route. While the Fugitive Slave Law meant that owners could recover escaped slaves in both free and slave states, slavecatchers were more aggressive in slave states, especially as prospects for a Confederate victory in the war seemed to be fading. The first leg would end with a crossing of the Susquehanna River into Pennsylvania. Upon arrival in Columbia, the party would be met by the local Vigilance Committee, which would prepare passengers for the next segment. This segment would proceed some 265 miles overland to Syracuse, NY. The third leg of the voyage would circle northwest around Lake Ontario to Toronto.

After his welcoming remarks, Inniss introduced the mission's conductors. "The lead conductor for this trip will be my good friend, Johnnie Jones," the reverend began, asking Jones to stand. "JJ, here, has led missions for us for more than ten years and has safely conducted many souls to the Promised Land. I have great confidence in him. Working with him will be Joshua Simpson, Solomon Johnson, and Wilson Rogers," Inniss continued, pointing to Joshua and Solomon as he introduced them. Rogers was not in attendance. "Joshua has worked with us on many previous missions. Solomon and Wilson are experienced conductors, but previously worked on other lines."

The burly JJ then stood to address the gathering: his work-clothes smudged with caulk after a long workday at the Navy Yard. He informed the group that the liberation train would depart Washington at 1:00 p.m. on Christmas Day, 1864, a date and time chosen because owners tended to somewhat relax restrictions on their slaves around holidays. He explained that slavers believed such gestures kept their "articles" in good spirits and motivated to remain compliant and productive. Thus, on certain holidays, they allowed visits to nearby spouses, children, and other family members who may have been sold or otherwise transferred to new owners. Of course, written passes would be required, as anyone in transit without them would be assumed to be contraband.

JJ went on to inform the group that on the first leg of the trip, passengers would be transported in two double horse-drawn carriages. Two conductors would drive the wagons and two would accompany them on horseback to observe traffic approaching from the rear and hopefully avoid unwanted interactions. JJ himself would drive the lead wagon. He explained that, although his intention would be to steer clear of violence, the conductors would be armed. He had talked privately to each of them to determine their willingness to carry and use weapons. All had agreed, and Solomon had volunteered to be one of the two mounted guards.

All nineteen passengers were to assemble promptly at the appointed departure time and date in the vacant lot two blocks east of Merrick's. There they would load carriages "appropriated" from one of the owners, Luther Wheeler, who farmed a large tract of land in Rockville. No luggage would be allowed, and only small backpacks could be carried.

Inniss informed the group that the nineteen proposed passengers would include four single men travelling alone, a single woman and her elderly mother, and three families, one a couple with three teenaged children, and two other couples with two small children each. Sensing that everyone was comfortable with what they had heard, the reverend asked that the few passengers in attendance introduce themselves and tell why they desired to travel north.

First to speak were John Wilson and his wife, Agnes, who claimed they were owned by "the meanest and cruelest man in Maryland." The owner of twenty-seven "head" of slaves on a farm just west of Annapolis, he tried to lower his costs by regularly stinting his slaves on food and clothing. Agnes had learned that the owner had creditors who might soon be coming after his assets. "He had already sold my brother to a planter in Mississippi," she added, "and there was no telling where we or our children might end up. When I heard from my cousin, who was part of the Wheeler headcount, that this voyage was being planned, I asked that we and our two children be included on the passenger list. That's why we're here."

The only other woman in attendance was next to speak. Wearing a torn dress and work boots that looked like something a man might wear to dig ditches or work in a mine, the young woman introduced herself. In a surprisingly robust voice, her words precise and well-articulated, she began: "I am Rebecca Williams. Two years ago, my husband was killed as he attempted to escape from the Georgia plantation where we were kept. Ten days later, I was sold when I resisted the lustful advances of my master. After I was imprisoned for sale, my mother, Vivian, attempted to find a purchaser in the neighborhood so that I could remain close to her and my two children. But in his vengeance, the master wouldn't allow the sale, and I was purchased by a new owner who traded me to Luther Wheeler. Fortunately, they considered my mother to be of no value, so they sent her along with me. But my children are still in Georgia.

"My new mistress," Rebecca continued, "is cruel to both me and my mother. Despite all the housecleaning work I'm hired out to do here at the Merrick Roadhouse, she allows me only two dresses a year, and she won't bring in care when my mother is ill. I must get out of here so that I can save my mother and figure out a way to recover my children. Hopefully, they're still at the same plantation."

Next to speak was William Hunt, one of the passengers travelling alone. William was owned by a Gaithersburg farmer named Townsend Dillard, who he considered a "moderate slaveholder." Although Townsend owned "twenty head of slaves," that he did not punish excessively, he had recently begun drinking heavily and behaving in erratic ways. In a drunken rage, he had recently threatened to kill one of his articles. William described how Dillard had blocked his efforts to find night work so that he could save enough money to buy his freedom. When William heard about the planned emancipation trip, he asked to be included.

The last of the five passengers in attendance was Eugene Spratt, who was also travelling alone. His story was simple. He was also owned by Luther Wheeler and under the supervision of Wheeler's wife, a mistress who "knew no mercy and offered no comfort." As soon as he heard about the upcoming escape from Rebecca, Eugene decided he would have to be on the train. He could no longer tolerate the domineering and cruel spirit of his owners.

After the introductions and a few additional words of welcome and assurance from Reverend Inniss, the group relaxed and enjoyed dinners that had been prepared in advance for them. Solomon was encouraged by the camaraderie that quickly developed within the prospective travelers. He enjoyed the few words he shared with each member of the travel party as the group mingled after finishing their meals. He couldn't help but notice Rebecca. Despite the awful circumstances of her life, the death of her husband, and the cruel separation from the children she hadn't seen or heard from in more than a year, she somehow projected strength and determination. In her conversation with her fellow travelers, she imparted words of encouragement and hope that were accompanied by an engaging smile.

With guidance and help from Inniss, JJ and his team spent the remaining evenings of December gathering and organizing the supplies and equipment required for the mission. Both two-horse wagons and the teams that would pull them would be taken from the Wheeler farm at 10:00 a.m. on escape day. The horses for Solomon and the other conductor riding lookout would be procured locally by Inniss. Three days of rations for each of the passengers and conductors would be packaged and stored at the Merrick facility in the final days prior to the mission.

Because of his White House guard experience, Solomon was tasked with assisting JJ to acquire pistols, rifles, and ammunition for the four conductors. JJ informed the team that as soon as he secured the armaments, likely from contraband sources, he would organize a "squirrel hunting" outing that would allow conductors to familiarize themselves with the weapons.

The weapons were procured the following week, and the four conductors assembled to test their guns at a small game hunting area just outside city limits. Solomon's riding and shooting skills, with both pistol and long gun, were immediately apparent, the result of many childhood hunting excursions with his father in Ohio. JJ and Joshua

Simpson were equally proficient, but Wilson Rogers, the eldest of the four conductors was only a fair shot and had an old leg injury that prevented him from riding a horse for an extended period. He was thus assigned to drive the second wagon.

When the group assembled for one last meeting on Christmas Eve, a distressed JJ informed the group that Joshua Simpson suddenly had taken ill and would not be able to travel with the mission. This meant that the group would have only three conductors and one mounted guard, Solomon. At this point, it was too late to recruit additional conductors. Not knowing how many skilled marksmen there might be among the passengers, Rev. Inniss cautioned the group that it would have to travel with maximum stealth to avoid armed confrontation and the likely superior firepower of pursuing slavecatchers. Even though only five travelers were in attendance, all nineteen had been alerted and would appear with two wagons at the appointed meeting place at 10:00 a.m. Christmas Day.

As Rev. Inniss prepared to end the meeting with a prayer for safe travels, Rebecca asked for permission to speak. She shocked everyone when she asked that she be allowed to ride along with Solomon as the second mounted guard. She informed the group that she was an accomplished horsewoman and a crack shot with both a pistol and a revolver, skills she had picked up as a child accompanying her master's children on hunting trips in which they amused themselves by competing with her in tracking animals and target practice. The children never admitted to their parents that, over time, their little slave playmate had honed the skills to outshoot them and any adults that chaperoned the outings.

Under normal circumstances, neither Inniss, Solomon, nor any of the other conductors would even think of expecting a woman to ride as an armed guard on a slave escape. But Rebecca's bold offer, delivered with a firm voice and a steely stare, was powerful and compelling. After a lengthy silence, Inniss announced to the stunned group that she would ride as the other mounted conductor. With a short prayer, the final escape planning meeting came to an end.

Christmas Morning was bright, sunny and cold. A light dusting of snow had fallen overnight. At 9:48 a.m., as two double-horse-drawn wagons pulled into the vacant lot near Merrick's, the last of the nineteen passengers arrived, an extraordinary accomplishment considering that so much of the trip organization and planning had been communicated to prospective travelers indirectly by word of mouth. Buoyed by their accomplishment, the travel party quickly loaded the wagons with provisions that had been stored at Merrick's.

At 1:00 p.m. sharp, the two wagons pulled out onto Allegheny Way. With Solomon and Rebecca on horseback behind the second wagon, the travelers began their journey to Columbia. The passengers were dead silent as the party braced itself to pass briefly through Maryland, the very slave state from which most of the travelers were escaping, and in which they would soon be pursued as runaways. The mood was grim as both passengers and conductors watched carefully throughout the day for any signs of the slavecatchers that were likely already pursuing them. Determined to retrieve not only the runaways but also the stolen horses and wagons, slavecatchers could be expected to administer serious, immediate punishment to all those apprehended and recaptured.

The only other travelers encountered during the long travel day were two one-horse carriages passing in the opposite direction, each with only a single passenger aboard. The tension eased when the party reached its first-day destination, a farm outside Ellicott City, a railroad train stop just west of Baltimore. Everyone relaxed and even shared conversation as soon as the travelers and wagons were safely inside Eli Thomas's barn and provisions were shared.

To stay ahead of pursuers, travel resumed before dawn the following morning. Shortly after leaving the Thomas farm, snow began to fall. No one complained about the poor visibility and bitter cold, however, as the harsh conditions would make slavecatcher pursuit more difficult. No other travelers were encountered throughout the day, and both wagons cheered when the party crossed the Pennsylvania state line. Although slavecatchers were now likely in hot pursuit, at least the party would no longer have to travel through slave-holding territory. Even Rebecca, who had been riding quietly and grim-faced with Solomon at the rear of the procession, finally allowed a small smile as the party pulled into its second stop, a farm on the outskirts of New Freedom, another railroad stop town. Conversation was livelier that evening as travelers spread out their sleeping bags in yet another barn, that of Ned Woods whose farm was a mile west of the city. But after a quick meal, lantern lights were soon extinguished in the barn. The stress of another day of illegal contraband travel had taken its toll on the party.

The third travel day began slowly. The additional snow that had fallen overnight had to be cleared so that the wagons could reach the main thoroughfare in front of the Woods farmhouse. By midmorning, the wagons were loaded and heading northwest. Under gray and overcast skies, the travel party proceeded slowly through snow-covered trails without incident, reaching the western shore of the Susquehanna River just before nightfall. As they neared the dock in search of the captain of the riverboat that was to transport them into Pennsylvania, three strangers on horseback approached. All were armed, their weapons visible but not drawn. Unlike the show of force by the intruders, the conductors' weapons could not be seen, pistols were holstered under their coats and rifles were stacked in one of the wagons.

One of the three strangers dismounted, walked to the front of the lead wagon, and asked where the party was headed. Seated on the wagon's front bench were JJ and Jenny Fisher, one of the escapees from the Luther Wheeler farm. Following a prearranged contingency plan, Jenny, a mixed-race daughter of Luther Wheeler's brother now posing as a white woman, responded that she was moving two wagonloads of furniture to her new home in Harrisburg, Pennsylvania. She identified JJ as one of the moving crew.

The trace of a sneer on his unshaven face, the stranger persisted. "Ma'am, my name is Seth Conklin. Me and my companions are in pursuit of two wagons and more than a dozen slaves that ran away from three different Maryland farms on Christmas Day. Since these here rigs pretty closely match the description of the wagons missing from the Wheeler farm, I hope you don't mind me lookin' at the furniture you're hauling and checkin' this boy's papers and the papers of these two on horseback."

As Conklin prepared to step up into the wagon, one of his fellow riders reached for a rifle holstered on his horse. When he cocked the unsheathed weapon, Rebecca drew her pistol and fired, hitting the stranger and causing him to slump forward on his horse. Solomon fired at Conklin as he scurried onto his horse. Conklin and the third rider attempted to return fire as they fled at a full gallop from the barrage directed at them by Rebecca, Solomon, and the other two conductors. The disabled intruder had fallen from his horse and laid lifeless at the side of the road.

The loud gunfire drew the attention of crew members from several boats docked at the pier. One was the captain of the *Carpenter*, the ship that was to transport Solomon's party to Pennsylvania. The more than one-mile crossing had been planned for the next morning, but considering the possibility that search party reinforcements might appear at any moment, all horses, wagons, and passengers were loaded, and the *Carpenter* pulled anchor.

It was not until the ship docked on the Pennsylvania shore that Solomon realized Rebecca had been wounded in the gunfire. When she stumbled on the gangplank, he noticed that her left sleeve was soaked in blood. She begged Solomon and the others not to overreact, as she didn't want what she called a "minor flesh wound" to delay the escape and prevent her mother from receiving the medical care she now badly needed.

"But your wound may be even more serious than your mother's condition," Solomon countered. "We know she's sick and needs care as soon as possible. But you've been shot and need care right away before you bleed to death," he continued, pulling her back aboard the *Carpenter* and into a small cabin.

After snatching off her jacket and ripping open the sleeve of her blouse, Solomon saw that the bullet had not lodged in her shoulder and no bones appeared to be broken. The bullet had passed all the way through. After frantically cleaning and bandaging Rebecca's wound with the alcohol and skimpy dressings found in the ship's medical cabinet, Solomon's tension began to ease, now that he knew the life of the brash young fellow conductor was not in jeopardy.

Upon the party's arrival in Columbia, the local Vigilance Committee found medical help for Rebecca and her mother. The doctors deemed Vivian fit to continue the second leg of the trip three days later but recommended that Rebecca stay in town a few days longer to recuperate. Her blood loss was significant, and she had contracted an infection. With that medical input, the committee arranged for Vivian to join the next group travelling to Syracuse and for Rebecca to resume her own travels one week later. Rebecca promised her mother that she would soon be joining her Toronto.

Solomon had planned to quickly return to Washington as soon as the travelers reached Columbia but decided to stay with Rebecca until she could safely resume her journey. He had always been troubled that he had never heard from his very first passengers, Cleo and her daughter, that they had safely reached their journey's final destination. He regretted that he may have left them too soon and didn't want to repeat the mistake with Rebecca.

To Solomon's relief, by the end of the week, Rebecca's fever had broken, her infection was gone, and her arm was no longer in a sling. Always a striking woman, her grim countenance had given way to frequent smiles. In the few weeks Solomon had known her, Rebecca seemed to have become both happier and more attractive. As she prepared to join the next travel party to Syracuse, she surprised him by suggesting that he join her, not only as a conductor but as a travel partner. She asked how she could not want to continue to travel with the man who had conducted her to safety and nursed her back to health after they had been together on the winning side of a gunfight. Though intrigued by the invitation and the prospect of continuing to travel with Rebecca, Solomon knew he had to return to Washington to secure the job and career he had worked so hard to initiate. Perhaps, at the right time and place, he and Rebecca might resume their friendship.

XII

The Plot

Abraham Lincoln

After a long workday at the War Department that included two hours of overtime, Louis Weichman arrived home in an agitated mood. For several days he had been hoping to see John Wilkes Booth and John Surrat at the boarding house where he took lodging. He knew the two planned to meet there sometime that week. He just didn't know which day.

The small hotel on H Street in the Northwest section of DC where Weichman roomed, was owned and operated by John Surratt's mother, Mary. As he sat reading a newspaper in a parlor near the front door, he fretted that both Booth and fellow lodger Surratt were shunning him. He had met Surratt when the two were seminary students at St. Charles College in Endicott City, Maryland.

A year after the outbreak of the Civil War, both left the seminary without becoming priests. Weichman taught school for a short period before coming to the District and beginning work at the War Department. Because of his friendship with Surratt, he took up residence at Mary Surratt's boarding house, an establishment that had long served as a Confederate safe house where escaped rebel war prisoners were moved from the North to Southern states. There he met Booth, Surratt, and several other secessionists. In recent months, the group had spent many hours discussing the war and their obsession, kidnapping President Lincoln and ransoming him for the release of Confederate prisoners of war. After Weichman learned that Booth and Surratt were both members of the Knights of the Golden Circle and were providing information about the movements of Union troops to the Confederacy, he began serving as their courier and passing messages between them.

Despite his support, Surratt and Booth had cooled on Weichman in recent weeks. They worried that he couldn't be depended on in a crucial mission. They believed he talked too much and might compromise their plotting with boastful comments to friends and coworkers about his involvement in what he labeled "important secret operations." In a confrontation earlier in 1864, Surratt had even ridiculed Weichman to his face about his ineptness in firing a weapon and riding a horse.

The longer Weichman sat waiting for Booth and Surratt to show up, the more he was convinced they were avoiding him. The old conversations he had enjoyed with them and other KGC members seemed to no longer occur. He felt he had ceased to be a part of the hotel's secret secessionist inner circle.

Weichman was correct. Booth and Surratt no longer trusted him and now avoided discussing their plans in his presence. The pair had decided to kidnap Lincoln and take him to Richmond, Virginia where they might be able to exchange him for Confederate prisoners. When Booth learned that the Union had ceased prisoner exchanges in response to the Confederates' refusal to return colored troops, he put the plan on hold. But he later reactivated it, concluding that recovering Lincoln would be so important to the Union they would proceed with an exchange even if colored troops were not included in the swap.

When they were able to access information about the president's March schedule, the two plotters settled on a kidnap date of the 17th, the day Lincoln's carriage was to return to the White House from a visit to Campbell General Hospital, a Union Civil War treatment center. But the plot was again aborted when Lincoln changed his mind about the visit and remained in Washington. Lincoln's change in plans coincided with an overall tightening of security that began after Solomon met with his former Light Guard Commanding Officer, told him of the seditious talk among War Department personnel, and related his conversation with Captain Gleason. Following that meeting, the president made no further solo walks to the War Building. He cut down on his carriage rides to the Old Soldier's Home and cancelled a planned open house at 1600 Pennsylvania Ave.

To a few inner circle members of his secessionist group at a dinner meeting that same month, Booth unveiled a new plan. It was common knowledge that Lincoln enjoyed the theatre. Since one of his favorite actors Edwin Forest was playing an engagement at Ford's Theatre, if Lincoln came to see Forest, perhaps he could be captured at the performance.

Booth's dinner companions didn't like the proposal. An isolated setting had always been deemed an essential element of a presidential kidnapping and extensive preparation had gone into an abduction in the country. Attempting to abduct Lincoln in a crowded theater seemed absurdly risky and impractical. Surrat labelled Booth's plan foolhardy and unworkable as it was widely known that the government was on full alert, its heightened concern based on intelligence warnings that a Confederate plot of some sort was afoot. Rumor had it that additional security fencing would soon be erected around the Capital complex.

Insulted that his new plan had been questioned, a sullen Booth sat wordlessly through the remainder of the dinner. When there was consensus that his abduction plans should be shelved for the moment, Booth erupted. Slamming his fist to the table, he exclaimed: "Well gentlemen, if worst comes to worst, I shall know what to do!"

Although it was not clear what Booth was threatening, no one was surprised at the overly dramatic outburst from the volatile thespian. One of the most popular and recognizable stage performers of the time, the young actor had an explosive temper and seemed always to have a chip on his shoulder. His impatient and resentful attitude could be traced, in part, to the beginning of the war when he wanted to put his acting career on hold to fight for the Confederacy but was talked out of it by his mother. The decision would eat at him and contribute to erratic and angry behavior for the rest of his life.

The dinner ended with harsh words and even threats of violence between Booth and other members of the party. But knowing that he still needed the group and that his passions might have caused him to overreact, he apologized, saying that perhaps he had drunk too much champagne.

Booth's angst and anger went further back than his failure to become a Confederate soldier. The ninth of ten children born to noted British Shakespearean actor, Junius Booth and his mistress, Mary Ann Holmes, John Wilkes was part of a family torn apart by the Civil War. Two of his brothers Edwin and Junius, Jr. were also actors, but there was intense rivalry and discord among the three. Like his father, Edwin had become a successful stage actor, performing primarily in the Northeast, home to many of the most lucrative venues. Not wanting competition from his family, when Junius Jr. and John Wilkes expressed a desire to begin their own acting careers, Edwin directed them to the West and the South respectively where they struggled to make a living, even though the hard-drinking John Wilkes enjoyed wide popularity. Resentments among the brothers were aggravated by their political differences. Edwin was a Lincoln supporter while Junius, though neutral, often disagreed with John Wilkes who supported slavery, hated abolitionists, and believed that Lincoln's election had been illegitimate.

Late in 1864, despite their many differences and frequent family quarrels, Edwin proposed that the brothers unite for a one-night production of *Julius Caesar*. Initially suspicious, John Wilkes later agreed. Even though the performance was interrupted by fires in a nearby hotel, the play was an artistic and financial success. Its theme of civil war, oppression, conspiracy, and assassination eerily forecasted soon-to-enfold events in Washington DC. Promoted by Edwin, the play portrayed the assassination of Caesar by Brutus as an act of heroism. Junius played Cassius, Edwin played the assassin Brutus, and in an odd casting twist, John Wilkes took the part of Mark Antony, who fought the assassins and drove them out of Rome.

In addition to its ominous *Art imitates Life* implications, the performance ended with several unexpected outcomes. Instead of distributing profits from the very successful show among his financially troubled brothers, Edwin infuriated them by donating the proceeds to the City of New York to erect a statue of Shakespeare in Central Park. It was also later learned that the fires that interrupted the performance were part of a Confederate plot to burn down the city. When John Wilkes expressed his pleasure at the news, Edwin put him out of his upscale New York apartment, and the two never again saw each other.

John Wilkes never quite got over the disappointment of the reunion. It only added to the sense of failure and shame he had always suffered not only because of his lost opportunity to serve in the Confederate Army, but because of the many other frustrations he endured throughout a life that began with illegitimate birth. The rejection of his kidnap plot by his fellow conspirators now pushed him deeper into depression and rage.

In November, Lincoln was elected to a second term in a campaign that pioneered the use of absentee balloting. Even though the new procedure had been implemented to allow soldiers to vote from the front, Booth and many other Confederate sympathizers saw it as a Republican power grab. They feared that Lincoln would use his war powers as a tool for what they perceived as ultimate destruction of society.

Despite his concerns about fading prospects for a Confederate victory, Booth had made little progress on his abduction plans. Drifting back and forth between New York and Washington, he rarely performed and instead focused on providing information to the Confederates on the movement of Union troops. Though he was rapidly depleting his meager savings, he began falsely boasting to associates that he was enjoying success as an oil speculator and investor. While in New York on one of his trips, he attempted to pump new life into his dormant abduction plan by purchasing armaments. He bought an assortment of carbines, Colt revolvers, and Bowie knives. He also purchased caps, cartridge belts, and several pairs of handcuffs. He arranged to have some of the items transported to DC by horse and buggy. The rest he packed and shipped by express.

Often using borrowed funds, Booth continued his abduction preparations even though no specific kidnap plans or dates had been set. In addition to firearms, he also acquired several horses, often with members of his secessionist group conducting the transactions. Assembling supplies and equipment in this manner personally involved each of the conspirators in the plot. This gave Booth a degree of control over the group and encouraged them to keep the mission secret. His collaborators firmly under his sway, the bitter thespian now waited for the optimum moment to execute the seizure.

XIII

Leader Down

The way to right wrongs is to turn the light of truth upon them.

Ida B. Wells

One month after Lincoln's inauguration to a second term, Robert E. Lee surrendered his troops at Appomattox. Although skirmishes would continue through May, on April 9, 1865, the Civil War was effectively over. With the firing of five hundred cannon shots, Washington DC lapsed into an extended jubilee party, with citizens crowding the streets and waving flags. Two days later, with a large and raucous crowd assembled in front of the White House, Lincoln gave an address from a window in the north portico. It would be his last.

The first to appear in the window was the president's twelve-year-old son, Tad. Amid cheers and shouts of approval, he waved a captured Confederate flag. When the president stepped to the window a few moments later, the assembled crowd erupted into unrestrained enthusiasm, everyone screaming with delight, many tossing their hats into the air, a nearby band playing "Yankee Doodle." Assembled in the room behind him were Mrs. Lincoln, several family friends, and a few members of the White House staff. Among them was Elizabeth Keckley. Solomon had just cut the president's hair and stood next to Mrs. Keckley.

As dusk settled in, several in the crowd called out for a light so that Lincoln could be clearly seen. A lamp was produced, and when Tad rushed to his father's side asking to hold the light, the president gave his approval, and Tad was handed the lamp. With the light shining fully upon him, Lincoln stood out starkly in the surrounding darkness as he waited patiently for the cheers below to end.

As those in the room stood quietly, Mrs. Keckley whispered to Solomon, a note of alarm in her voice: "What an easy matter would it be to kill the president, as he stands there! He could be shot down from the crowd, and no one would be able to tell who fired the shot."

The president then began his remarks with somber words of hope and prayer.

> We meet this evening, not in sorrow, but in gladness of heart. The evacuation of Petersburg and Richmond, and the surrender of the principal insurgent army, give hope of a righteous and speedy peace whose joyous expression cannot be restrained. In the midst of this, however, He from Whom all blessings flow, must not be forgotten. A call for a national thanksgiving is being prepared and will be truly promulgated.

After thanking General Grant and the many brave Union soldiers who helped secure victory, the president spoke on the delicate topic of readmission to the Union of former secessionist slave states. He spoke of how, in 1863, he had announced *The Ten Percent Plan* for reconstructing Confederate states under Union control. According to the plan, he would pardon Confederates and readmit to the Union any state in which at least ten percent of eligible voters swore an oath of allegiance and the state agreed to abolish slavery. The plan called for, but did not require, Negro suffrage.

Many Republicans thought the plan too lenient since it did nothing to the end the economic and political dominance of the planter class and did not adequately protect the rights of ex-slaves. Lincoln used his address to state his support for readmission of Louisiana to the Union since some twelve percent of eligible citizens had voted in favor of allegiance to the Union. Even though he expressed his disappointment that the percentage voting in favor was low, and that the state's vote did not include provisions for the colored vote, the president expressed his belief that the immediate readmission of the state was an important step to full restoration of the Union.

In the crowd in front of the White House listening intently to every word uttered by the president, John Wilkes Booth was shocked and disgusted to hear Lincoln publicly express his full support for Negro suffrage. To a fellow Surratt-house secessionist listening to the speech with him, Booth erupted. "That means nigger citizenship. Now, by God, I'll put him through!" he exclaimed as he angrily pushed his way through the crowd and out into the street.

Later that evening, Booth stopped at Ford's Theatre to pick up mail that the venue regularly accepted for him. He was more furious than ever at the thought of losing any of the liberty and privilege he enjoyed as a white man because of freedoms newly granted to Negroes. To several theatre employees in the box office, Booth fumed: "We are all slaves now! If a man were to go out and insult a nigger now, he could be knocked down by the nigger, and nothing would be done to the nigger!"

As the sharp-tongued performer was not a favorite of the theatre staff, one quickly shot back, with a smirk: "Then, you should not insult a nigger."

With the war now over, Booth could no longer fantasize about abducting the president and arranging a prisoner trade. After releasing some of his frustrations with a long walk down Pennsylvania Avenue, Booth stopped at the Surratt boarding house where he encountered John Surratt, Louis Weichman, and a few of the remaining members of his abduction team. Over drinks, he lamented about how he had squandered opportunities to kill the president, both at his recent inauguration and again that night, when on both occasions he stood only a stone's throw from him. "At the inauguration, I was on the stand as close to him nearly as I am to you. And at the victory speech tonight, I stood right below the window from which he spoke.

I vow that I will not waste another opportunity!"

"You're crazy, John. What good could that do?" admonished his old friend and fellow thespian, Sam Chester, one of the boarding house secessionists. "The war is over, and the Confederacy is dead."

"If I eliminated the Black Republican leader," Booth snapped, "I would live in history! This is not over."

When Chester reminded him that there should be enough glory in a successful stage career, Booth answered: "I'm done with acting. The only play I would even consider at this point is *Venice Preserved*." No one picked up on Booth's oblique reference to the plot of the eighteenth-century play, the assassination of the leaders of Venice.

On April 11, an article in the District's *Evening Star* newspaper reported on a resolution adopted by the City Council the day after Lee's surrender:

> That in view of the surrender of General Lee and his whole army to Lieutenant General Grant, and the assurance which it gives of a speedy restoration of the Union, the citizens of Washington are hereby earnestly requested to manifest their rejoicing in this glorious event by illuminating their private residences, places of business, and all the public buildings on Thursday night, the 13th instant, beginning at 8 o'clock.

In early April, Lincoln had begun to experience premonitions of his own death. On April 12, he told his good friend and sometimes bodyguard Ward Hill Lamon about the most recent occurrence. He described a dream in which he wandered the White House searching for the source of mournful sounds:

> I kept on until I arrived at the East Room, which I entered. There I met with a sickening surprise. Before me was a catafalque, on which rested a corpse wrapped in funeral vestments. Around it were stationed soldiers who were acting as guards; and there was a throng of people, gazing mournfully upon the corpse, whose face was covered, others weeping pitifully. 'Who is dead in the White House?' I demanded of one of the soldiers, 'the President,' was his answer; 'he was killed by an assassin.'

Earlier, the president had told his cabinet of a dream in which he was on a "singular and indescribable vessel that was moving with great rapidity toward a dark and indefinite shore." He described to them that he had repeatedly had the same dream before "nearly every great and important event of the War," events such as Union battle victories.

⸻⚬⸻

General Grant arrived in Washington the morning of the thirteenth. Word had it that he and his wife would be celebrating the *Grand Illumination* that evening at the National Theatre in the company of the Lincolns. Upon learning of the planned presidential celebration, Booth rushed to the National and asked the manager whether it was true that the president and his party would be in the building that evening. He was elated at the confirmation. An assassination on April 13, would be perfect, he immediately thought, as killing the president was now more than ever his patriotic duty. Believing that the fate of the nation hung in the balance, he concluded that a public execution would heighten its impact as would the historical significance of the date. Not only was the thirteenth the birthday of Thomas Jefferson, the author of the Declaration of Independence, it was also the day of reckoning on the Roman calendar—*The Ides of March*.

With his actor's sense of drama, Booth decided that he would further add to the historical significance of the assassination by modelling it on the killing of Caesar. The National Theatre offered a public and highly visible place for such an important event. The Derringer he would use had been made in Northern Liberties, a Philadelphia neighborhood, and the dagger he would carry was inscribed with the words: *America, land of the Free*. In this, his greatest performance, he would deliver, in Latin, the line: "Thus always to tyrants!"

Consistent with his notion of a Caesar-inspired assassination, Booth believed that Lincoln could not be his sole target. Just as Mark Antony pursued and defeated the emperor's assassins, Booth feared that he might also face retribution from Lincoln loyalists such as Secretary of State William Seward. Convinced that Seward was a power-hungry extremist, Booth decided that he too would have to be killed. To complete the elimination of Republican tyranny and decapitate the Union government, Vice-President Johnson would also have to be eliminated.

Having decided that he would kill Lincoln himself, Booth met with conspirators Lewis Powell, John Atzerodt, and David Herold and secured commitments that Powell would execute Seward and Atzerodt would deal with Johnson, both at their homes. Since Powell was unfamiliar with Washington, Herold would guide him to the Seward house and then rendezvous with Booth. According to Booth's plan, the killings should occur simultaneously, with the executioners then leaving Washington and meeting up across the river in Maryland. The mission would employ the weaponry and horses that Booth had earlier assembled.

To Booth's disappointment, the Lincolns did not attend the illumination with General Grant that night. The president cancelled and stayed home with a severe headache. But the next day, Booth got word from Ford's Theatre that a White House messenger had come to the theatre to reserve a box that evening for the president, Mrs. Lincoln, and several guests to see the play *Our American Cousin*.

The Lincolns arrived at the theatre the evening of April 15, some twenty minutes after the beginning of the play. Several who had originally planned to attend with the Lincolns were missing. Among the no-shows were Ulysses Grant and his wife who did not get along with Mary Lincoln. Suffering with a headache, Mrs. Lincoln, herself, was reluctant to attend but agreed to accompany the president since the press had been notified that the first couple would be in attendance.

As the Lincolns made their way through the audience, the play paused while the band struck up *Hail to the Chief* to a full house. As he and his wife entered their private box, accompanied by their guests for the evening, Lincoln acknowledged the band's salute and the applause of the audience with a bow. As the play resumed, Booth climbed the stairs to the dress circle and unobtrusively made his way to the president's box. The night before, he had written in his diary, "Our cause being almost lost, something decisive and great must be done." The time had now come for him to fulfil his destiny. Booth and Lincoln had never met, but the president had earlier seen Booth at the theatre and admired his work. He had invited the actor to the White House, but the invitation was never accepted.

A White House guard stationed at the door to the box recognized the actor. When Booth handed him a business card and asked to be admitted into the box, the guard allowed the actor to pass without searching him for weapons. Booth then closed and barred the door behind him. Now in a small passageway, he edged toward an inner door leading out to the box. There he waited in the dark, his Derringer in one hand and his dagger in the other, Lincoln seated just a few feet ahead of him. Through a peephole in the door he had bored earlier in the day, Booth was able to observe the president and his party as they watched the play. He knew the play well and waited to take his shot simultaneously with audience laughter at a humorous line upcoming in the play.

No longer feeling the calming effects of the whiskies he had nervously downed at a bar next to Ford's, and his heart now pounding, Booth burst into the box as the audience erupted into laughter, placed his pistol at the back of the president's head, and fired. The bullet entered Lincoln's skull behind his left ear and passed through his brain, causing him to slump over in his chair, surrounded by a cloud of smoke.

Jolted by the gunshot, one of Lincoln's military guests lunged at Booth, who slashed him with his dagger, inflicting a deep wound. With a final glance at the mortally wounded president, Booth dropped his pistol, planted a hand on the box railing, and bolted over it, landing on the stage some twelve feet below. In the frenzy and pandemonium that followed, Booth headed for a door at the back of the stage that led out to an alley behind the theatre. But before leaving the stage, Booth turned, faced the audience, raised his dagger, and defiantly shouted: "Sic temper tyrannis!" Somehow avoiding capture, he made it out of the theatre, leapt into the saddle of his getaway horse, and headed for the Maryland border.

Booth's easy escape from a theatre crowded with hundreds of onlookers, many of them soldiers, after shooting the president in plain view, was probably enabled by the audience's confusion. Many recognized the flamboyant actor and thought his attack was fake and an impromptu play for attention, or perhaps that it was part of the performance as Booth was known as a very athletic and fit artist. In any case, he was gone from the theatre before most of the large audience realized that the president had been shot.

When a young army surgeon in the audience reached the presidential box and examined Lincoln, he quickly determined that the president's wound was mortal. The fallen head of state was transported to a private home across the street from the theatre and laid diagonally across a bed for which he was too tall. With little hope he would recover, a team of doctors attended the unconscious president throughout the night, attempting to remove blood clots and make him comfortable. Several cabinet officers and officials rushed to the president's bedside and kept vigil through the night, but the wounded leader never regained consciousness. When he was pronounced dead at 7:22 the next morning, Secretary of War Stanton proclaimed, "Now he belongs to the ages."

Although Booth's attack was successful, the other assassins did not achieve their goals. At 10:15 p.m. on the night of the attack, as Booth made his way to the Ford's Theatre presidential box, Lewis Powell knocked at the front door of Secretary Seward's home. He was able to gain entry under the ruse that he was delivering medicine from Seward's physician and that his instructions were to show Seward how to take it. At the Secretary's bedroom door, Powell fought with, and overpowered, Seward's suspicious son. He then rushed to Seward's bed, slashing him in the face and neck. Seward miraculously escaped death when a protective cast from a recent accident prevented Powell from administering a fatal blow. David Herold had guided Powell to the residence but ran off after hearing the fighting inside the house. Powell was able to get out of the house, but being unfamiliar with the city, was soon apprehended.

At that same moment, George Atzerodt was to have gone to Vice President Johnson's room at the Washington Hotel. But the burly conspirator stopped at the hotel's bar for a drink and ended up drunk. After throwing away his weapon without ever encountering Johnson, he too was arrested.

Fleeing Ford's Theatre, Booth was able to cross the Navy Yard Bridge into Maryland where he linked up with Herold and hid for several days near the Zekiah Swamp. While in hiding, he recorded in his diary his shock at the widespread condemnation of his actions. The actor had expected to be celebrated as a hero. After securing weapons previously stored in a Maryland safe house, and stopping for Booth to receive treatment for a broken leg he sustained escaping from the theatre, they made their way to the Virginia farm of a former Confederate Army officer who was a friend of Booth's.

On April 26, after a nationwide manhunt, soldiers from the 16th New York Cavalry surrounded the barn where Booth and Herold hid. Herold surrendered, but when Booth refused to give himself up, the barn was set afire. As he tried to escape the blaze, Booth was shot and killed.

Most of the other conspirators were captured by the end of April. After a lengthy military tribunal, Powell, Atzerodt, Herold, and Mary Surratt, proprietor of the Surratt boarding house, were convicted of murder, sentenced to death, and hung. Other conspirators received prison sentences of varying lengths, and a few were even acquitted. John Surratt escaped to Europe, many years later to be captured, tried, and acquitted.

The president's assassination unleashed a flood of public mourning in the North, the South, and from around the world that began the next day, Easter Sunday. The sense of loss was particularly strong among citizens of color who had celebrated Lincoln's fight to end slavery. Black and white churches were packed to capacity with crowds spilling out onto streets, some mourners too far away from the pastor to hear words of prayer and condolence. In US Army camps, Union soldiers gathered in chapels, barracks, and parade grounds to mourn the loss of the beloved leader. Frederick Douglass, speaking in Rochester, New York, the day after the president's death, told a large crowd that because of his race, he felt the loss "as a personal as well as a national calamity."

International mourning for the esteemed president led to the issuing of a special edition of the *Foreign Relations of the United States*, a US government periodical that normally published only routine diplomatic correspondence. But on this unusual occasion, only condolences for Lincoln were included. In an earlier edition, Lincoln had urged the US to recognize Haiti and Liberia, two nations that had also fought slavery. The US recognized both nations in 1862. Within this issue, a Liberian proclamation mourned a man who "was not only the ruler of his own people, but a father to millions of a race stricken and oppressed." It proclaimed that Lincoln had "died to redeem a nation, a race," and that "generations yet unborn shall call him the mighty ruler, the great emancipator, the noble philanthropist." The Haitian Legation in the United States denounced the assassination as a "horrid crime," claiming that the attacks on Lincoln and his cabinet that "have thrown the whole United States into consternation and mourning, will everywhere excite the same wail of sorrow and condemnation."

After public viewing in both the White House and the Capitol, Lincoln's body was taken on a thirteen-day train journey across the country to his home in Springfield, Illinois. As part of his homegoing, the president's remains were transported in a horse-drawn hearse along 5th Avenue in New York City.

Despite the punishment of the conspirators, as the nation attempted to move past the twin tragedies of an insurrectionist war and the killing of a president, it exhibited a strangely forgiving attitude toward the leaders of the failed secession. As members of the Confederacy attempted to resurrect their images through the myth of the Lost Cause, the remainder of a grieving but still racially divided nation hoped to never again experience such misfortune. Many were optimistic that, despite its recent trials and tribulations, the wounded republic might come together. They were hopeful that the nation might finally achieve the goals proclaimed but never fulfilled by the founders, that all citizens could enjoy the fundamental rights of liberty, equality, and free speech.

XIV

Behind the Scenes

Every great dream begins with a dreamer. Always remember, you have within you the strength, the patience, and the passion to reach for the stars to change the world.

Harriet Tubman

The White House staff was deeply moved by the president's assassination. Among the many who mourned his loss, Elizabeth Keckley was particularly touched. Although her primary inspiration to write her book had been to tell the extraordinary story of her rise from slavery to the highest circles of business and government, she also wanted to pay homage to the *Great Emancipator* who had freed her people. She also wanted to help her close friend, Mary Todd Lincoln. Having served as Mrs. Lincoln's dressmaker and confidant from the time she arrived in Washington through the remainder of the president's time in office, she knew the first lady had been devastated by the murder of her husband, and earlier, the by the death of three of her four sons, two as children, one, Willie, while her husband was president.

Mrs. Keckley had always been touched by Lincoln's spirituality and how he took strength from reading scripture. The vicissitudes of war and the changing fortunes of the Union Army frequently depressed the president. On those occasions it was his practice to seek comfort in the Bible. In her book, Keckley tells of one particularly dark day when the Confederates had enjoyed a series of battlefield victories. She describes the dejected president drawing strength from reading about Job.

> I almost imagined that I could hear the Lord speaking to him from out of the whirlwind of battle: 'Gird up thy loins like a man: I will demand of thee, and declare thou unto me.' What a sublime picture was this! A ruler of a mighty nation going through the pages of the Bible with simple Christian earnestness for comfort and courage and finding both in the darkest hours of a nation's calamity. Ponder it, O ye scoffers at God's Holy Word, and then hang your heads for very shame!

Within the pages of *Behind the Scenes*, Keckley expressed a foreboding about imminent danger she had always believed the president faced. She was especially troubled the first time she ever heard him address the public, his speech from the window above the White House front entrance the day the Confederacy surrendered. Keckley later shared her concern with the first lady, who acknowledged that the president's life had always been in danger. Mrs. Lincoln had lived in constant dread of a tragedy and always feared that her husband would meet with a sudden and violent end.

After the president's assassination, Mary Lincoln found herself heavily in debt. The former first lady tried to raise money by selling her jewels, furs, and gowns, but her efforts were brutally attacked in the press, in stories such as one in the *Columbus Sun* that labeled her as a "mercenary prostitute." Keckley knew Mary to be a generous, loving person and believed that if the public knew more about her, it would judge her more charitably.

But Keckley completely misread the situation—both the public resentment of Mrs. Lincoln, and how her own efforts to write and speak on her friend's behalf would be received. The former first lady had already alienated citizens of color with her refusal of aid from Negro leaders such as Frederick Douglass who wanted to raise money to assist the beloved president's family after his assassination. But Mary's snub also caused problems for Keckley. To many, her support of the ungrateful first lady made her a traitor to her race.

Behind the Scenes was not well received by the public. The poor reception was a surprise to both Keckley and her publisher, as several previous slave narratives, such as those by Frederick Douglass and Josiah Henson had been published earlier and received well by the public. These stories had been adopted and promoted by abolitionist causes and had advanced the careers of the authors. Douglass's book, no doubt, played a part in his becoming a diplomat and a US Ambassador. In recent years, other White House memoirs had also been popular.

Whether through publisher incompetence or malicious intent, the narrative penned by Mrs. Keckley was not what was published. Her manuscript was edited to include nothing of her autobiography. Instead, the finally published book, was more of a tell-all about White House goings-on during the Lincoln administration than it was a former slave's autobiography. To make matters worse, Keckley had provided her publisher with letters Mary had written to her. Although she had instructed the publisher that comments of a personal nature were to be deleted, the letters were printed in full.

In her book, Keckley was unfailingly flattering to the martyred president who she viewed as a great leader and a humble man of service. On a personal level, she had always appreciated Lincoln's friendly demeanor and the respect he accorded her. A courtly and gracious gentleman who doffed his high hat to greet women and men alike, the president always referred to her as Madame Keckley.

Although Keckley was supportive of Mrs. Lincoln and had written of her in compassionate terms, she was perhaps too frank in descriptions that made the first lady appear to be petty, jealous, and envious of others in Washington political circles. Worst of all, in her efforts to accentuate Mary's dire financial situation, she inadvertently portrayed her as an undisciplined and profligate spender who kept her debts secret from her husband.

For someone as careful and deliberate about her own personal affairs as Elizabeth Keckley, it was hard to imagine how she had not anticipated that Mary Lincoln and others in Washington society might be offended by the disclosure of Lincoln family personal details, especially since she knew the first lady to be short-tempered, and prone to grudges and resentment. Because she was such a strong-willed, exceptional person who had already broken many racial and gender barriers, Keckley's self-confidence might have led her to believe she could be totally frank in her writing and entrust a publisher with the sensitive task of editing Mrs. Lincoln's personal letters, some of which were explosive. It was a serious error.

Public reaction to the book was immediate and devastating. While other White House tell-alls had not been challenged as ghostwritten, *Behind the Scenes* was immediately labeled as such, with literary critics leading the assault. Newspapers condemned it as "indecent literature" and as "trash and scandal." The *New York Citizen* labeled Keckley a "servant girl," and charged not only that the book was full of lies, but also that she could not have been the author.

Keckley had had her own worries about how the book would be received, but never expected the relentless, devastating attack that would come her way. She had been concerned mainly that people might find her too forgiving of the slave owners and the families she had served during her slave years. She was also worried that with the war now over, some readers might resent having to hear, once again, about slavery and its evils. She didn't think a few personal details about the Lincolns would be viewed negatively but was concerned that her gender might be a problem, as few outspoken women had a voice in the public sphere at the time.

The public uproar seemed to be focused on the tell-all aspect of Elizabeth's book, even though nothing was disclosed that suggested betrayal of public trust, dereliction of duty, or other serious scandal. The public resented the very notion that a woman, especially a woman of color, would have the audacity to think she could speak out in such a frank manner about the affairs of a white woman. Keckley had violated accepted norms and stepped out of her "place." Mary Lincoln even turned on her, issuing negative comments about her and the book.

Even though things were never quite the same for her after her book was published, Mrs. Keckley moved on with her life. Later, she would accept a position as head of the Wilberforce Domestic Science Department where she would once again enjoy a measure of public respect. But it would be generations before her trailblazing achievements would be fully recognized and appreciated.

XV

So Far Away

If thus, we by the grace of God, live up to this our Profession; we may cheerfully go the rounds of the compass of this life, having lived according to the plumb line of uprightness, the square of justice, the level of truth and sincerity. And when we are come to the end of time, we may then bid farewell to that delightful Sun and Moon, and the other planets, that move so beautifully round her in their orbits, and all things here below, and ascend to that new Jerusalem, where we shall not want these tapers, for God is the Light thereof; where the Wicked cease from troubling, and where the weary are at rest.

Prince Hall

In the final months of the Civil War, Solomon had assisted in a few additional Underground Railroad missions. But his fondest UGRR recollections were those of the transport that took the St. Mary's travelers to freedom. Upon their safe arrival in Canada and her reunion with her mother, Rebecca Williams had written him, describing her new life in Toronto as a seamstress, the home she shared with her mother, and her desire to somehow reconnect with her children.

Solomon responded, telling Rebecca how the war was progressing toward a Union victory. He also told her how the friendships he had made on the mission prompted him to join St. Mary's. He cautioned her about venturing south to rescue her children, reminding her that, as their prospects for victory in the war faded, Confederates had become more vicious in their treatment of escaped slaves.

Confident that the coolheaded and determined escapee who had helped him fight off slavecatchers would be able to protect herself in all situations, Solomon was devastated to receive word, two weeks after the president's assassination, that Rebecca had been killed in a failed attempt to rescue her children from the Atlanta plantation to which they had been sent. The shocking news came to him in a letter from her mother.

Vivian Williams
2-234 Spruce St. N
Toronto ON M5V 1J2

Solomon J. Johnson
3d West N.
Washington DC

April 22, 1865

Dear Solomon,

It is with great sadness that I write to tell you of the death of my precious daughter, Rebecca. She was killed three days ago as she attempted to rescue her children from captivity in Atlanta. I am trying to arrange for her remains to be sent to me here in Toronto so that we can give her a proper homegoing. Knowing how fond she was of you, how much she appreciated your assistance in our escape, and how you had tried to convince her not to attempt a rescue at this point in the war, I thought you would want to know about this terrible loss. We both appreciated your bravery, and I will forever be indebted to you for the safe passage you ensured. As soon as funeral arrangements are made, I will contact you with details.

Sincerely,
Vivian Williams

Although Solomon had only known Rebecca for a short time and in the most stressful of situations, he was crushed to think that she was forever gone, and even worse, that she had perished in an attempt to save her children. She had been taken away far too soon. Solomon had never been even close to intimacy with Rebecca or any other woman, but at the moment, he suddenly felt lost and alone. He thought he might find closure by visiting Vivian Williams in Toronto and paying his final respects to Rebecca. But he cancelled his plans when he learned, the night before his departure, of the death of Robert Jenkins, the Foggy Bottom hackney with whom he had bonded on the Eliza Cobbins escape. Robert had been killed a few days earlier when the wagon in which he was transporting passengers to Silver Spring, was intercepted by slave-catchers.

The ensuing weeks were a blur for Solomon. He had been struggling to shake off the blues that had gripped him since the tragic death of a leader with whom he had developed a deep bond of respect, affection, and appreciation. Now, with the passing of Rebecca and Robert, only the demands of his wartime work at Treasury kept him from lapsing into a state of deep depression. Like many young men, he had focused on carving out a career for himself and making his mark on the world. Before he met Robert, he had never seriously considered membership in Masonry. And before he crossed paths with Rebecca, it had not occurred to him how much his world might be enriched with the right partnership. What a cruel irony, he thought, that the people who had awakened him to such new possibilities would never be able to share them with him.

Solomon began attending St. Mary's on a regular basis, finding comfort in the surroundings that had so profoundly changed his life. He had developed an attachment to Reverend Inniss, and Church member John Cook, whose father was the founding pastor of nearby Fifteenth Street Presbyterian Church. Solomon had first met Cook when the future Prince Hall Grandmaster visited the White House as part of the Negro delegation that discussed colonization with the President. Since he only saw his family on the occasions he could get away to Ohio, he appreciated the new bonds he was forming at the church, among them, new ties to a group of the younger members of the congregation who met regularly to discuss the challenges of wartime survival, the integration into society of newly freed slaves, and management of the grief associated with the loss of loved ones.

The traumatic experiences discussed in group sessions helped Solomon understand that he was not alone in his anguish. Over time, he found healing in the compassionate listening and support of fellow group members. Providing that same nurturing to others helped him overcome his grief and regain a semblance of optimism. Most other members of the group also found the mutual sharing of compassion and support to be helpful and healing.

As summer began, Solomon began to feel the need for a visit to Columbus. He missed his mother's cooking, and he had unfinished business with his father. On Friday, July 14, he arrived home with plans for a family celebration of his twenty-first birthday the next day. That evening he enjoyed an impromptu gathering at the nearby home of one of his close friends who had called together several of the Columbus group with whom he and Solomon had grown up. Solomon enjoyed relaxing and reminiscing with his old friends, most of whom he had known since childhood. A new member of the group was Elizabeth Cunningham, an attractive young woman who had moved to Columbus from Virginia with her family shortly after he had departed for Washington with the Union Light Guard. Having lived the last few months with the melancholy of too many deaths, Solomon found the warmth and good cheer of the get-together, particularly that of the charismatic Elizabeth, to be the perfect tonic.

<hr>

"Dad, can we talk about Masonry?" Solomon asked Hanson as they completed a hearty breakfast the next morning. "I've always admired your Masonic dedication and the good works done by your lodge under your leadership," Solomon began as the two stepped into Hanson's small study.

"Although I've not previously been interested in joining the order, my feelings have changed. Despite all the good works of lodges like yours, I never understood why Prince Hall Masons separated themselves from white Masons. I understand the importance of race pride, but it never made sense to me that Negroes would want to be a part of an organization but not strive for full membership. If Masonry is so racist, I always wondered why men of color would want to be a part of it in the first place. By separating themselves from white Masons, it always seemed to me that black Masons limited their power and reach and lost the ability to utilize the vast resources of mainstream Masonry."

"I've heard some attempt to justify Prince Hall Masonry by equating the separation of Negroes and whites in Masonry to the separation of the races in America," Solomon continued. "But to me, there's a big difference. Negroes never chose to come to America and separate themselves from it. Because we were brought here in chains, we had no say about whether we could participate in the American dream. But in Masonry, it always seemed to me that Negroes chose to join an organization that didn't want them. Once they worked their way in through European lodges, they separated themselves. It made no sense."

After pausing to refill his and his father's coffee cups, Solomon concluded: "I've only recently come to appreciate how colored men would want to be part of a such storied and historic order that was established to achieve honorable spiritual and service goals."

"Now you've got it," Hanson quickly responded. "That was our motivation. It was only when we understood that white Masons would never allow us full membership that we separated. Instead of begging European Masons to provide us with charters to operate lodges here in the US only to be labeled as "clandestine" by white US lodges, we separated to become Prince Hall Masonry."

"But regardless of Prince Hall Masonry's origins," Solomon continued, "it's clear to me I've been focusing on the wrong things, looking backward instead of forward. I'm now understanding why you've always said that Masonry is a work in progress. At this point, I'm focusing more on the order's present good works and opportunities than its past issues. I've seen much of that good work in Washington."

After a long thoughtful pause, Hanson responded: "Son, I can only say I'm happy to see how you have grown and matured, and how you now view the world from a more thoughtful perspective. And, of course, I still stand ready to welcome you into Masonry. I believe you will find it fulfilling, and I'm sure you will be a great asset to the craft.

"After a bloody Civil War and the assassination of a president," Hanson continued, "America stands at a critical juncture. Prince Hall Masonry can play an important role in the nation's survival, but we need the talents of young thinkers and future leaders like you. My lodge will soon form a group to receive the first degree of Masonry, and I believe you will make a good candidate. At our next meeting this Thursday, it will be my great honor to submit your name for consideration. I'm confident the response will be positive.

"In October," he added, "Candidates will be trained and initiated as Entered Apprentices in a first-degree ceremony. The following month, they will be passed to the Fellowcraft, second-degree level, and in November raised to third-degree Master Masons. If you decide to proceed, and I hope you do, you'll have to come up to Columbus for each of the degree ceremonies. After that, you can either remain a member of this lodge, or you can demit to a lodge down in DC or anywhere else in the world your travels should take you. But even if there is no local lodge for you to join, you will still be a Mason. We believe that a Mason is not necessarily a member of a lodge, but rather one who daily tries to live the Masonic life and intelligently serve the needs of the Supreme Architect of the Universe."

Two days later, Solomon was back in Washington, making his rounds at Treasury. But his mind was on Masonry and the opportunity to finally join his father in the ancient fraternal order. As soon as he received word that he had been approved to take his first degree, he made arrangements to return to Columbus for the ceremony. Tuesday evening, Sept 19, he sat in an anteroom adjacent to the main meeting room, the Blue Room, on the second floor of the stately lodge hall, a Blue Lodge of Master Masons where the three degrees of Masonry were conferred.

Tonight, the lodge had been called to order in the first degree to initiate candidates as Entered Apprentices. At precisely 8:30 p.m., the lodge's Secretary and its Junior Deacon entered the anteroom clad in black suits, white gloves, and their distinctive Masonic aprons. Following a series of questions asked by the Secretary and answered satisfactorily by the ten candidates, the Junior Deacon ordered the candidates to adjust their clothing in preparation for and in accordance with the initiation ritual. He then led them, single file, into the Blue Room. Solomon was awestruck by the stately chamber, its Masonic accoutrements, its blue walls and ceiling, and its black and white checkered marble floor. All windows were covered to prevent eavesdropping, and the single entryway was guarded by the Tyler of the lodge who was armed with a sword. Master Masons clad in aprons and white gloves were seated on benches at both sides of the room.

Seating for lodge officers was intricately arranged. At the east end of the room on an elevated platform sat the Worshipful Master also clad in apron and gloves, but in addition, wearing a black silk high hat. Out of deference and respect for his leadership and the inspiration he provides, the master is always seated in the east, the direction from which the sun rises. Several past masters of the lodge, including Hanson Johnson, sat behind him.

On the left of the Master sat the Secretary, on his right the Treasurer and the Senior Deacon. At the west end of the room, on the other side of a centrally located altar sat the Senior Warden who was next in line to become the master. The Junior Deacon was at his side. The Junior Warden sat on the south side of the chamber.

The secret initiation ritual began with prayers at the altar and several recitations as candidates were led around the Blue Room past the Master, other officers, and the rest of the craft. Each word spoken, each movement and gesture of the ceremony participants appeared to be prescribed. Situated before the three principal officers of the lodge, the Master, Senior, and Junior Wardens, were small podiums, gavels atop them that were rapped from time to time to initiate or conclude segments of the ceremony. Several in the side benches read silently from coded books, following the highly ritualized procedure, step by step. The small manuals were entitled: *Ecce Orienti or Rites and Ceremonies of the Essenes.*

The highlight and conclusion of the ceremony was a recitation by the candidates, in union, of their Obligation, their pledge and commitment to Masonry. The solemn process was completed in slightly more than one hour with all ten candidates successfully initiated into the first degree. It was an evening that would be remembered forever by the new Entered Apprentices. Following an October second degree passing to the level of Fellowcraft, Solomon was raised to the third degree of Masonry on November 21, 1865. He was now a Master Mason.

Although he had been initiated into the Columbus lodge, Solomon began meeting informally with several other colored Masons living in Washington DC who had no current local affiliations. Among them was Amos Jackson, one of the Mt. Zion Guild members he had teamed with to conduct Eliza Cobbins and her daughter Cleo on the first leg of their journey to freedom. Over occasional dinners, the young Masons discussed lodges they might wish to visit or possibly join. They also talked about the need for colored Masons to focus attention on the particular challenges faced by Negroes at the end of the war, the need for education, employment, and voting privileges. They hoped to find a lodge willing to expand its attention beyond the traditional emphasis on spirituality and the provision of assistance to Masons in distress. They agreed that Masons should continue to prioritize these important long-established issues and concerns. But they also agreed that Prince Hall Masons could and should help address current needs of the broader colored population.

As the ad hoc Masonic group continued their meetings to plan lodge visits and discuss public service initiatives they hoped to support or possibly even initiate, their attention was drawn to the Freedman's Bureau, a federal agency established during the short-lived Reconstruction period to provide freed slaves with food, clothing, and temporary shelter. Its additional goals were to help rebuild the nation, reintegrate the former Confederate states, and address the social, political, and economic impacts of slavery. The Bureau was authorized to dispose of confiscated Confederate land by leasing or selling it to freedmen in forty-acre parcels. Most importantly, it established freedom schools to teach ex-slaves to read and write—skills considered critical by the freedmen themselves as well as by the government. Through this assistance, freed slaves began voting, forming political parties, and assuming stronger positions in employment situations with their former masters. But with meager government funding, Bureau training services depended on donations and partnering with third-party community service organizations such as black churches.

Despite the benefits it provided to freedmen, the Bureau was unable to operate effectively in certain parts of the country, mostly in the South. Its nemesis was the Ku Klux Klan, which terrorized former slaves for trying to vote, hold political office, or own land.

Because of his daily travels through the War Department, the parent agency of the Freedman's Bureau, Solomon had heard of the many freedmen's hospitals that served sick, undernourished victims of slavery, and of the churches that provided training in support of freedmen's schools. Fascinated by their work, he had read through available documents that described the challenges faced by the bureau and the stories of the people it served. He particularly enjoyed reading about the reconnection of families that had been separated by slavery. After sharing his insights with his Masonic colleagues, the group decided to support the activities of one of the churches, Tolson's Chapel, a black church located near the Antietam Battlefield in Maryland. Solomon's group sought a local lodge that might work with them to raise funds and perhaps provide instructors to support the Tolson training initiative.

Working through an existing lodge did not prove fruitful. Fundraising was minimal through the one lodge that agreed to participate, and no trainers were recruited other than two volunteers from the ad hoc group itself. At their most recent get-together, they discussed the problem and the growing awareness that the local lodges they had visited showed little interest in combining traditional Masonic activities with war-related emancipation support services to the community.

Several of the Fraters knew of such involvement in lodges outside the DC area. When he was working with Robert Jenkins on the Eliza Cobbins mission, Solomon remembered Robert telling him about how his Boston lodge not only operated an Underground Railroad Line but also provided cover in the lodge for escaped slaves waiting for transport. Although the Underground Railroad had never received formal Masonic support or acknowledgement, many Masons and, in some cases, entire lodges had operated stations. Lodges in some states even operated under the name North Star Lodge, appropriating the title of the ultimate destination of all Underground Railroad lines, the North Star, UGRR terminology for freedom. In one Illinois lodge that took this name, all the founding lodge officers happened to also be the conductors that created the local North Star UGGR line.

"Although the membership of most of the local lodges we've visited includes brothers of all ages, I'm sure everyone has noticed that the leadership is usually the more senior members," Solomon began at their most recent meeting. "These men are good Masons, but they view the Masonic mission in somewhat narrow, almost parochial terms. To them, the order is focused entirely on Masons themselves, their families, their widows, and orphans. They believe that the principal duties of the Master of the Lodge are to 'raise its living and bury its dead.'

"But the world is changing so quickly," he continued. "It doesn't make sense to limit our mission to only the scope of issues that was relevant in the Middle Ages when the order was born. Who says we can't be mindful of both traditional Masonic principles and current issues facing the broader community?"

"I agree with you, Brother Johnson," Walter Ridgeway responded, "and other than the Tolson School initiative, I can't imagine a crisis that more urgently needs the collective strength and muscle of Masonry than working to secure righteous behavior from a nation that hovers between continuing the enfranchisement of Negroes and sliding back into oppression.

"Should we build on Civil War gains by pushing to provide education to Negroes and expand voting rights?" he asked. "Or should we do nothing and allow the clock to be turned back with payment of reparations to former slaveowners but not to former slaves, and by charitably forgiving the white supremacists who supported the assassination of the president who brought change? Will we allow Andrew Johnson to abolish the Freedmen's Bureau and end the Negro vote? Worst of all, will we simply stand by and watch the growth of hate groups like the Ku Klux Klan, which has begun a ruthless campaign of intimidation and violence directed at black freedmen, Northern schoolteachers, Freedman's Bureau officers, and Republican Party supporters?

"Although it is clear the goal of most reconciliation supporters is the reestablishment of white supremacy and the stifling of politically active Negroes like us, they cloak their backsliding under the heroic mantle of the Lost Cause myth.

"It is hard to believe," Ridgeway continued, "that more than one hundred years after America's original sin of the kidnapping and enslavement of Africans, with the nation not even one year into a righteous attempt to reform itself and address the injustices suffered by our race, the country is once again divided. The biggest concern of the new president is that Reconstruction not punish or humiliate the insurrectionist Southern states that seceded from the Union. It's clear that racists and bigots have crawled out from the rocks under which they had been driven and are intent on restoring white supremacy and putting us back in our place."

Rising to emphasize his point, Ridgeway challenged his Masonic companions: "I know you men are aware that before the Emancipation Proclamation, the 'three-fifths' rule meant that the slave-holding states could only count three-fifths of their enslaved population to determine how many representatives they could send to Congress. But are you aware that former slaves are now counted as full persons even though they can't vote? Because of the resulting 'increase' in their population count, Southern states may end up with more congressional representation than they had before the war! There are estimates that they may pick up as many as thirteen representatives, and we can be sure that the additional votes will not support any legislation beneficial to us. It's hard to imagine a more perverse twist on the punishment the South deserves for its treason. After nearly achieving equality, it seems clear that the US is backsliding and will once again fail to achieve the full promise of its own Constitution."

"We're faced with some unbelievably tough challenges," Solomon responded, "and we must continue the fight. But we must be realistic.

We're a handful of unaffiliated Masons, so there's only so much we can do right now. To address one piece of the problem, the need for education, I recommend that we continue working through existing lodges to support the Tolson Church training initiative as best we can. Perhaps we might also organize a letter-writing campaign to lobby congress to expand Negro voting rights here in the District.

"If we want to expand our involvement in emancipation-related activities, we will either have to ascend to leadership positions in an existing lodge or form a new lodge. Since neither of those options is going to happen quickly, in the interim we will have to work independently as an ad hoc group."

As the nation's commitment to postwar reconstruction waned under the leadership of a president determined to reconcile with and support the rehabilitation of former Confederate interests, Solomon and his group continued to assist the Freedman's Bureau in its various programs. Sometimes working with local lodges and sometimes working independently, they raised funds for the Tolson training program through such activities as raffles and solicitation letters sent to private citizens and local businesses. Several of the group also volunteered as Tolson instructors.

They were gratified and encouraged when they learned in the Fall of 1865 that their support was contributing to the opening of the Storer School for Negroes. The facility would be located in nearby Harper's Ferry, a community that Frederick Douglass had referred to as 'the town where the end of American slavery began.' Situated at the eastern Tip of West Virginia where the Potomac and Shenandoah Rivers meet, the Harper's Ferry arsenal had been destroyed during the war and never rebuilt. The town was in poor condition, but a vacant building that had once been a Union general's home had been converted into classrooms.

Storer would begin by providing the basic skills of reading, writing, and arithmetic to formerly enslaved freedmen and their families. Establishment of such a school at the end of the Civil War exceeded the group's own expectations, as education of slaves was potentially a capital offense in some states. The education of free blacks was forbidden by law in many areas.

When a Maine philanthropist provided a $10,000 grant to match start-up funds provided by the Freedman's Bureau, several local Baptist Churches, and other donors, including Solomon's Masonic group, the new school was born. It was chartered as "a school that might eventually become a college, to be located in one of the Southern states, at which youth could be educated without distinction of race or color." The school began with a class of nineteen formerly enslaved children and a few of their parents, sometimes with children and parents in the same class.

Though it eventually became a college, for decades Storer was simply a normal school that provided high-school-level instruction to future primary school teachers. For twenty-five years it would be the only school in West Virginia where a person of color could get an education beyond the primary level. For many, the school was an embodiment of the Bible verse which proclaims that "God will make a way where there is no way." Solomon and his Masonic allies would always be proud of their involvement in its founding.

XVI

Elizabeth

I am not tragically colored. There is no great sorrow dammed up in my soul, nor lurking behind my eyes. I do not mind at all. I do not belong to the sobbing school of Negrohood who hold that nature somehow has given them a lowdown dirty deal and whose feelings are all hurt about it. Even in the helter-skelter skirmish that is my life, I have seen that the world is to the strong regardless of a little pigmentation more or less. No, I do not weep at the world—I am too busy sharpening my oyster knife.

Zora Neale Hurston

A few days after his Third Degree Masonic ceremony, Solomon received a congratulatory card from Elizabeth Cunningham. He wasn't sure how she knew his address but was happy to receive the handwritten card in which she expressed her pleasure in having met him that summer and her hope that their paths might cross again sometime soon. His prompt and enthusiastic response generated a cycle of frequent letter exchanges between the two.

When he disclosed that, in order to overcome the impact of the loss of several important people in his life, he had become actively involved with a church discussion group that grappled with wartime survival issues, she confided that she too was struggling with depression brought on by the recent loss of several older family members and the earlier death of two young neighbors who died on the same day in the Battle of Antietam, the deadliest one-day battle in American military history. The two teenaged brothers lived on the same street as Elizabeth and had been in the army barely three months when they were cut down in Sharpsville, Maryland during an infantry attack on Confederate defenders. "They were barely old enough to enlist," Elizabeth wrote Solomon. "But weren't they also children of God? How could they have been taken so soon? And so many other boys just like them were lost that same day," she continued. "Many survived the day but left the battlefield missing an arm or a leg, or perhaps sightless, never again to see the faces of loved ones. Where is the justice in any of this?"

"If there is any justice in the brutality of war," Solomon responded in his next letter, "it is beyond human understanding. Perhaps it is part of God's will or some other master plan. We may never know. But what we do know is that life is fragile and can end at any time. We must make the most of each day, as we can never be sure which one will be our last."

As Elizabeth and Solomon slowly overcame their mourning through letter exchanges, their friendship grew. As they learned more about each other's hopes, fears, and dreams, they discovered that they had once met as children years ago when Elizabeth and her family had visited relatives in Columbus before moving to the city. Having frequently discussed the fragility of life and how assumptions about longevity cannot be made even among the young, the two survivors began sharing further details about their lives.

The more the two corresponded and the more frequently Solomon returned to Columbus, the more he appreciated Elizabeth's charisma, intelligence, and conversational skills, attributes she usually kept in check as did many well-bred young women of the era. But Solomon began to see her as a woman ahead of her time, possessed of skills and interests that many would deem inappropriate for a postbellum lady who had been raised to believe that her purpose in life was to become a wife, mother, and homemaker. While he had no problem with domestic roles, for either a man or a woman, he began to appreciate how such role expectations and limitations might have caused Elizabeth to limit her horizons.

Keeping a lid on her dreams and ambitions had, in fact, taken its toll on Elizabeth. To family and friends, she often appeared incommunicative, at times even unapproachable. The day Solomon met her, she was attired in a floor-length dress, the front of which was adorned with a double row of buttons that ran from the bottom hem up to the high collar. He had never seen so many buttons on one garment. In the coming months he noticed that many of her garments had a similar button treatment. He began to associate her attire with what seemed to be a "buttoned-up" disposition. He wondered whether her seemingly repressed nature might somehow be linked to societal limitations of her soaring ambitions, her inquisitiveness, and her desire to create. When he finally knew her well enough to mention his observations about her attire, she brushed off his observations, attributing the button overload to merely a style quirk. Solomon wasn't convinced, but it didn't matter.

As Elizabeth and Solomon grew closer, they felt the need to share more than letter writing and Solomon's visits to Columbus. They got their first opportunity to enjoy an extended visit with each other when Elizabeth's family planned an Easter visit to relatives in Kentucky, and she accepted Solomon's invitation to spend the weekend with him and his family in Columbus.

Solomon's and Elizabeth's parents had also met some years ago but were not close friends. Elizabeth met Solomon's parents for the first time when her father and mother dropped her off at the Johnson residence on Holy Saturday morning, 1866. After introductions to his parents and his youngest two brothers who still lived with them, Elizabeth joined Solomon's mother in the kitchen and the two struck up an easy conversation.

Their relationship off to a good start, Elizabeth asked Solomon's mother whether she could assist with meal preparations. Susannah accepted the offer, and the two spent the afternoon chatting as they prepared the Easter Sunday meal. The next day's repast was festive and flavorful with after-dinner conversation stretching late into the evening. Elizabeth retired to the guest bedroom in good spirits that night, appreciative of how well Solomon's family welcomed her.

Hanson was not ready to end the evening, however, and invited Solomon into his den to continue their conversation over brandies.

"I like this girl," Hanson began. "You two seem to get along well."

"She's special and you're right, we do get along very well. When we met last June, we were both going through a rough patch. We helped each other through our troubles, and we've been very close ever since. Pretty much inseparable even though we're in separate cities."

"I knew you were troubled by the president's passing and the loss of your fellow Underground Railroad teammates. I'm glad you and Elizabeth were able to help each other. Mutual support is important in any good relationship."

"True, but we're also compatible in many other ways. She's smart and dreams big. I relate to that because I believe I inherited those same attributes from you. Even though she knows that, as a woman, there are many doors not open to her, she shares my ambitions and wants to help me achieve my goals. She believes that if I achieve, we both achieve. She's also very family oriented and likes kids, just as I do."

"So, it sounds like you two are a great pair. But that's right now. What's it going to be like in twenty years when the newness has worn off and you've had to survive some of the tough times that are an unavoidable part of life and every relationship? How do you know you will grow together and sustain the bond you now share?"

"That's a tough question, Dad," Solomon responded after a long and thoughtful pause. "How can any couple predict the future or know that they will grow together and not apart? I can only say that Elizabeth and I have already experienced some tough times together. If we can do it once, we can do it again. And maybe it takes some luck. The kind you and Mom have enjoyed. Whatever it is, I'm ready to roll the dice with Elizabeth."

"I like the way you're thinking, son. Of course, there are no guarantees about anything in life. When it comes to relationships, we can only try to choose a mate we love and know well, someone with whom we are willing to work to keep our bond strong. I think you and Elizabeth can do it. You have my blessings."

On his next trip to Columbus, Solomon proposed marriage to Elizabeth, assuring her that he would do everything in his power to help her achieve her own goals, not only as wife and mother, but in any other endeavor she chose to pursue. Elizabeth accepted immediately, and the couple began planning their wedding. They agreed that the ceremony would take place in Columbus at St. Paul's African Methodist Episcopal Church, the oldest AME church in Columbus and long the place of worship for both of their families. Six months later, surrounded by family and friends, they cemented their earthly bond, and a few days later, were on their way to Solomon's new quarters on Massachusetts Avenue in NW Washington DC.

Having spent her early years in Virginia, Elizabeth adjusted easily to the move to Washington with Solomon, and in early 1867, their first child, William, was born. Prior to their son's birth, Elizabeth and Solomon had visited and attended services at several churches. Solomon had hoped that St. Mary's Episcopal would be their permanent church home, but Elizabeth was unsure. As they prepared for William's baptism, however, they had to make a choice.

Solomon knew that Elizabeth was smart and inquisitive and that she preferred to fully understand an issue before making important decisions. But she surprised him with the research she had done on DC churches and the depth of her understanding of religious issues facing postwar churchgoers of color. In Columbus she had long attended

Bethel African Methodist Episcopal Church. Organized in 1823, it was the oldest Negro congregation in Columbus. From the time her family had moved to Ohio from Virginia, it had been committed to the mission of the AME, the first independent black denomination in the United States. It had been founded by the influential Negro leader Richard Allen when he called together the five colored congregations of the Methodist Episcopal Church to escape discrimination within the church. Elizabeth had always valued the AME commitment to advance the civil and human rights of Negroes through social improvement, religious autonomy, and political engagement.

While she appreciated St. Mary's, Solomons home church, the oldest Negro Episcopal congregation in the city, she had always been troubled by the denomination's past discriminatory practices. She knew how Negro churches had organized after the Civil War when colored parishioners would no longer allow themselves to be restricted to the balconies of existing Episcopal and Methodist Episcopal churches. But since no AME church had yet been established in Washington DC, she agreed to join St. Mary's and have William baptized there.

"I know you would have liked to have the baby baptized at an AME church here in Washington, one that could become our family church home," Solomon said to Elizabeth over dinner the evening she told him she would be agreeable to having William baptized at St. Mary's. "And I so appreciate it that you didn't let the choice of a church become a point of friction between us. I would have been happy to go to whatever church you chose whether or not it was St. Mary's. But I'm also happy that you feel comfortable attending my church. Most of all, I feel so lucky that you and I are together."

XVII

Black Codes

I have often been asked, how I felt when first I found myself on free soil. And my readers may share the same curiosity. There is scarcely anything in my experience about which I could not give a more satisfactory answer. A new world had opened upon me. If life is more than breath, and the "quick round of blood," I lived more in one day than in a year of my slave life. It was a time of joyous excitement which words can but tamely describe. In a letter written to a friend soon after reaching New York, I said: "I felt as one might feel upon escape from a den of hungry lions." Anguish and grief, like darkness and rain, may be depicted; but gladness and joy, like the rainbow, defy the skill of pen or pencil.

Frederick Douglass

On May 1, 1866, a large group of black soldiers, women, and children gathered on a Memphis Street for an impromptu street party. The black soldiers, all members of the Third United States Colored Heavy Artillery Regiment had been mustered out of the army on

April 30 but had to remain in the city for several days while they waited to receive their discharge pay. The army had taken back their weapons, but a few of the former soldiers had acquired their own. When police were called in to break up the celebration, the soldiers refused to disperse. The four responding officers were outnumbered and had to retreat as they called for reinforcements. The soldiers gave chase, gunfire broke out, and one officer was killed.

Triggered by news of the confrontation, mobs of white policemen and residents rampaged through colored neighborhoods and destroyed the homes of freedmen. In the three-day frenzy of violence following the confrontation, scores of black soldiers and civilians were attacked and murdered, and many acts of robbery and arson were committed.

Federal troops were called in to end the violence, and peace was restored three days later. A subsequent joint Congressional Committee investigation and report described the carnage. As expected, Negroes suffered most of the injuries and deaths, by far. Forty-six black and two white people were killed, almost two hundred were injured or robbed, and five black women were raped. Property damage was extensive, including ninety-one homes burned. The four churches and eight schools burned accounted for the destruction of every church and school in the black community.

Freedmen's Bureau investigators concluded that the May 1 confrontation was the result of long-term resentments caused by wartime occupation of the city by Union soldiers. With the complicity of local police, judges, and other municipal officials, Tennessee developed its own version of the Black Codes already in force in many other states. Struggling with worker shortages due to slaves escaping to freedom behind Union lines, slaveholders no longer had the benefit of free, forced labor. Whites resented the many freedmen in Memphis. The local military was directed to take into custody Negroes deemed vagrants and to force them to accept labor contracts on local plantations.

The new codes clearly exposed the harsh plans of Southern whites for former slaves, plans that were totally unjustified based on the outcome of the Civil War and the national mood. Freedmen might have had more rights than before the war, but they still did not have voting rights or citizenship. They could not own firearms, serve on a jury in a lawsuit involving whites, or move about without employment.

Under the codes, black women were particularly vulnerable. They were often the victim of sexual assaults by their white employers, as convicting a white man of such a crime in the South was almost impossible. Aggravating the problem was the perception among whites that black women were sexually avaricious and possessed of little virtue. At the same time, black men were thought to be sexually aggressive. Their supposed threat to the vulnerability and purity of white women served as justification for castration and lynching.

The primary goal of judicial systems in the South now seemed to be the coercion of

people of color to comply with the customs and labor demands of whites. Negroes accused of crimes were rarely able to secure legal representation, and their trials were usually discouraged unless conviction had been predetermined.

The Memphis office of the Freedmen's Bureau pushed back and questioned local officials about their racist policies, writing:

> How is it that the colored children in Memphis even *with their spelling books in their hands* are caught up by your order and told that they 'had better be picking cotton.' Is it for the purpose of conciliating their old rebel masters and assisting them to get help to secure their cotton crop? Has it come to this that the most common rights of these poor people are thus to be trampled upon for the benefit of those who have wronged them all their days?

The codes outraged most of the country, as it seemed clear that the South was creating a new form of slavery to negate the outcome of the Civil War. Members of both Congress and the Freedman's Bureau were flooded with citizen complaints. Public anger prompted a congressional investigation headed by a former Union general now serving in Congress. His report documented the illegal killing of thousands of former slaves. It concluded:

> The number of murders and assaults perpetrated upon Negroes is very great; we can form only an approximative estimate of what is going on in those parts of the South which are not closely garrisoned, and from which no regular reports are received, by what occurs under the very eyes of our military authorities. As to my personal experience, I will only mention that during my two days sojourn at Atlanta, one Negro was stabbed with fatal effect on the street, and three were poisoned, one of whom died. While I was at Montgomery, one Negro was cut across the throat evidently with intent to kill, and another was shot, but both escaped with their lives. Several papers attached to this report give an account of the number of capital cases that occurred at certain places during a certain period of time. It is a sad fact that the perpetration of those acts is not confined to that class of people which might be called the rabble.

Public reaction to the report came quickly in a flood of citizen complaints to Congress and to individual representatives. In the Washington DC area, a grassroots public-opinion campaign mounted by Solomon's Masonic group helped spur those complaints. They used newspaper articles and appeals at local churches to raise public consciousness about the onerous codes, and they generated their own letters to key House members.

The Honorable Thaddeus Stevens
House of Representatives
Washington, DC 20515

Dear Mr. Stevens:

We the undersigned write to you as Prince Hall Affiliated Masons in the Washington DC area. We respectfully request that you and your Congressional colleagues take immediate action to prevent the enactment and enforcement of Black Codes. These codes are onerous local rules, laws and regulations usually, but not exclusively, promulgated in former slave states. They illegally infringe upon the rights of black Americans, specifically ex-slaves.

Codes vary from locality to locality, but the following elements of the South Carolina Code are typical components of such illegal restrictions in most states:

1. **Civil Rights** – Restrictions on the Civil Rights of citizens that limit the rights of persons of color to acquire, own and dispose of property; to make contracts; to enjoy the fruits of their labor; to sue and be sued; and to receive protection under the law in their persons and property.

2. **Labor Contracts** – Rules stipulating the rights and obligations of employers and employees, who, in some cases, were referred to as *master* and *servant*. Black servants usually had to reside on the employer's property, remain quiet and orderly, work from sunup to sunset except on Sundays, and not leave the premises or receive visitors without the master's permission. In South Carolina, Masters could "moderately" whip servants under 18 to discipline them.

3. **Vagrancy** – Rules intended to pressure freed-men to sign labor contracts. These rules usually allow vagrants to be arrested and imprisoned at hard labor. Law enforcement authorities are then allowed to "hire out" black vagrants to a white employer to work off their punishment.

4. **Apprenticeship** – Black Codes provide another source of labor for white employers—black orphans and the children of vagrants. Courts are often able to apprentice such black children, even against their will, to an employer until age 21.

5. **Crime and Punishment** – Many Black Codes establish a racially separate court system for all civil and criminal cases that involve a black plaintiff or defendant. They allow black witnesses to testify in court, but only in cases affecting "the person or property of a person of color." Crimes that whites believe freedmen might commit, such as rebellion, arson, burglary, and assaulting a white woman, usually carry harsh penalties. Most of these crimes result in the death penalty for blacks, but not for whites.

6. **Miscellaneous Restrictions** – Other rules that reflect the white obsession with controlling former slaves. They usually ban black people from possessing firearms, making or selling liquor, and coming into the state without first posting a bond for "good behavior."

We humbly request that all such codes be immediately outlawed, and that the Freedman's Bureau be empowered to enforce compliance and initiate legal action upon violators.

Sincerely,

Walter O. Ridgeway

Solomon J. Johnson

Robert Connors

James Wiggins

Benjamin L. Jones

Delbert M. Thomas

In response to the public outcry, Congress enacted the Civil Rights Act of 1866, the nation's first such legislation. Its opening lines pronounced:

> All persons born in the United States ... are hereby declared to be citizens of the United States; and such citizens of every race and color, without regard to any previous condition of slavery ... shall have the same right in every State ... to make and enforce contracts, to sue, be parties, and give evidence, to inherit, purchase, lease, sell, hold, and convey real and personal property, and to full and equal benefit of all laws and proceedings for the security of person and property, as is enjoyed by white citizens, and shall be subject to like punishment, pains, and penalties and to none other, any law, statute, ordinance, regulation, or custom to the contrary notwithstanding.

President Johnson vetoed the bill, disturbed that it conferred citizenship on freedmen at a time when all Southern states had not yet been fully restored in Congress. He claimed that passage of the act would be a "stride toward centralization and the concentration of all legislative power in the national government." Although the Democratic Party, identifying itself as the party of white men of the North and South supported Johnson, Congressional Republicans overrode the veto, and the bill became law.

Although the Masons had no way of knowing the impact of their campaign, they were elated when Congress not only passed the Civil Rights Act but enacted an additional bill to continue the activities of the Freedman's Bureau. While the two pieces of legislation created new safeguards to ensure the rights and freedoms of former slaves, they did not provide all black citizens with the right to vote. Freedmen would not enjoy full suffrage until the passage of the Fifteenth amendment in 1870.

While entire black communities throughout the nation were jubilant at the passage of the Civil Rights Act and renewal of the Freedman's charter, reaction in Washington to Masonic lobbying was mixed. Community leaders were most appreciative. Masonic leaders also welcomed the legislation, but they directed Solomon and his group to refrain from inferring Masonic endorsement for any future initiatives unless approval was provided by the Grand Lodge and appropriate member lodges.

XVIII |

Transition

I, too, sing America.

I am the darker brother.

They send me to eat in the kitchen

When company comes,

But I laugh,

And eat well,

And grow strong.

Tomorrow,

I'll be at the table

When company comes.

Nobody'll dare

Say to me,

"Eat in the kitchen,"

Then.

Besides,

They'll see how beautiful I am

And be ashamed—

I, too, am America.

Langston Hughes

The Andrew Johnson Administration dimmed the hopes of many that the reforms of Reconstruction would continue or that former slaves might finally be able to live the American dream. Under the new president's direction, a modified version of Reconstruction was implemented. Although he issued a series of proclamations requiring seceded states to hold new elections and reform their local governments, he allowed them to return many of their old leaders to office and implement oppressive Black Codes. But Congressional Republicans pushed back, refusing to seat legislators from recalcitrant states and advancing legislation to overrule Southern actions. Johnson vetoed their bills but after Republicans overrode him, he went on a national tour to promote his policies and break his opposition. Congress responded by passing the Tenure of Office Act which limited the former Vice President's ability to fire executive-branch officials.

Despite President Johnson's foot-dragging and what appeared to be an effort to sabotage full Reconstruction, there were positive signs. Slavery had ended, and despite the efforts of many to limit freedoms of former slaves and block opportunities for black workers, progress was evident, even within Andrew Johnson's conservative Democratic administration. Following Solomon's hiring as the government's first black office worker, additional workers of color were hired for non-domestic office duties. After almost two years as a Treasury Department messenger, Solomon set his sights on a clerical position. Noticing that several such positions in Treasury were unfilled following the manpower demands of the war, Solomon applied for one of the open positions. Although no formal departmental directive had been issued to fill the position, he took the initiative and requested a promotion. Honing his correspondence skills, he submitted his request in a letter to the Secretary of the Treasury.

TREASURY DEPARTMENT
February 8th, 1867

Hon. Hugh A. McCulloch
Sec'y of the Treasury

Dear Sir,

Having been employed in the dept for more than three years.

Within that time I discharged my duty with satisfaction.

I most respectfully ask that an appointment be given me equal that of a first class Clerk in the Office.

I made the application in this brief manner to avoid offence and infringement. If this should meet with disapproval, I earnestly hope it will not create any dislike for me, but trusting to your kind disposition. I desire this will meet with your kind and favorable consideration.

I am with great respect

Your humble servant,
Solomon Johnson
Messenger

In the customary formality of the times, both the Secretary and his assistant provided written responses to Solomon's request. The day following Solomon's request, Assistant Secretary William Chandler scheduled him to appear before the Board established for the examination of Clerks in the Office of the Secretary of the Treasury. Immediately following the examination, Secretary McCulloch notified Solomon that he had been found qualified to perform the duties of a Clerkship in the

First Class and had been appointed a Clerk of that Class in the Secretary's office.

By the time he received his promotion, Solomon had joined a Masonic Lodge in the District. Several of the others who had teamed up with him to fight the Black Codes also joined. Proud of their effort, the feisty young Masons began lightheartedly, but privately, referring to themselves as the Black Code Fraters, and later simply as the Fraters. Several, like Solomon, were out-of-state transplants who now wished to establish more permanent Masonic roots in Washington. To do so, there could be no further rebukes from the Grand Lodge for taking political stances in the name of Masonry without proper authorization.

Solomon had also joined a related Prince Hall entity, the Simons Grand Commandery of Knights Templar. The Simons Commandery was open to Prince Hall Freemasons and was modeled on the historical Knights Templar. The organization's aims were to carry on the public service spirit of the original knights. They did so by organizing fundraising activities to support medical research and provide educational assistance to Masonic-related youth groups. On Dec 17, 1866, Solomon and Elizabeth celebrated their marriage and Solomon's promotion with a Knights Templar Social and Musical Entertainment charity benefit at Rothchild's Garden on Capitol Hill.

The years following Solomon's marriage would be busy and rewarding as he worked diligently to solidify his position as the Treasury Department's first black clerk, and share, with Elizabeth, the joy of family life. They had recently celebrated the birth of their first son, William. James, Solomon, Beatrice, and Jennie would be welcomed into the family over the next nine years.

To augment his Treasury Department $1,200 per year salary, compensation that was respectable but not adequate to properly support his growing family, Solomon continued to barber several evenings per week at District of Columbia Tonsorial Services, serving the circle of customers he had cultivated at the White House. Continuing also to read law at Howard University, he would finish his studies in 1872 and thereafter carry the distinguished LL.D., Doctor of Laws symbol of accomplishment after his name. In the remaining time, he continued his Masonic career, joining the newly formed Pythagoris No. 9 lodge in 1871 and beginning his advancement through the various Deacon and Warden chairs. In 1876, he would reach the East and be installed as Worshipful Master.

While Solomon was happy in his work and family life, and gratified with his Masonic and educational activities, his demanding schedule began to take a toll on him. Though he had never suffered serious health problems and thrived on an active lifestyle, from time to time he now had trouble sleeping and frequently experienced fevers and night sweats. At first, he ignored the situation, but when he lost weight and began experiencing frequent coughing spells, Elizabeth convinced him to see the family doctor, James Lawrence, who tended to their children. While he pronounced Solomon reasonably fit, Dr. Lawrence urged him to cut back on commitments and get more rest and fresh air. He set up monthly appointments to monitor Solomon's symptoms and progress.

Solomon was deeply unsettled by the troubling assessment of his health, an unwelcome dose of reality and an unexpected signaling of his mortality. Barely out of his twenties, he had always met past challenges with determination and a can-do attitude. No amount of hard work could prevent him from achieving his goals. Now he would have to modify his lifestyle.

An unexpected upside to Solomon's diagnosis was Elizabeth's reaction. If he followed the doctor's recommendation, he would have to modify his heavy work schedule. He worried that if he cut back on his work, his family might suffer. But Elizabeth shrugged off those concerns, assuring him that his health was now the family's primary concern. Even if it became necessary to pare down their expenditures and make more use of hand-me-downs to keep their children clothed, it was a challenge she welcomed.

Elizabeth's supporting and nurturing reaction was a tonic to Solomon. It affirmed and deepened his bond with her and infused him with new determination to achieve his dreams for the family, even in the face of his new limitations.

XIX

The Death of Reconstruction

We hold these truths to be self-evident, that all men are created equal, that they are endowed by their Creator with certain unalienable Rights, that among these are Life, Liberty and the pursuit of Happiness.

Declaration of Independence

The year 1865 had been a crucial year for the nation as it grappled with the loss of a president, recovery from the most brutal war in US history, and passage of laws to improve conditions for freed slaves. The Thirteenth Amendment to the Constitution, passed in 1865, had abolished slavery and involuntary servitude except as punishment for a crime. Disappointed with President Johnson's conciliatory approach to the South and his failure to administer proper punishment for secession, Congress reversed all his decisions relating to Reconstruction and would later impeach him in 1868.

Among the most egregious of Johnson's actions was his failure to enforce Confiscation Acts, laws passed by Congress during the war to free slaves and seize other Confederate assets. Even worse was his reversal of Union General William T. Sherman's Special Field Order No. 15, of January 16, 1865, a massive land redistribution program that confiscated 400,000 acres of land along the Atlantic coast of South Carolina, Georgia, and Florida previously owned by Confederate planters and provided it, in forty-acre parcels, to some 18,000 newly freed slaves. Popularly known as the *Forty Acres and a Mule Policy* and widely celebrated by people of color throughout the country, the multi-part order had been issued by Sherman at the end of his victorious March to the Sea as the Civil War neared its end. The order was conceived at meetings between Sherman, Secretary of State Stanton, and Negro leaders in Savannah, Georgia, the general's headquarters at the end of his March. The order stipulated that:

> The islands from Charleston, south, the abandoned rice fields along the rivers for thirty miles back from the sea, and the country bordering the St. Johns River, Florida, are reserved and set apart for the settlement of the Negroes now made free by the acts of war and the proclamation of the President of the United States.

> ... no white person whatever, unless military officers and soldiers detailed for duty, will be permitted to reside; and the sole and exclusive management of affairs will be left to the freed people themselves, subject only to the United States military authority and the acts of Congress. By the laws of war and orders of the President of the United States the Negro is free and must be dealt with as such.

> ... each family shall have a plot of not more than forty acres of tillable ground ... in the possession of which land the military authorities will afford them protection until such time as they can protect themselves or until Congress shall regulate their title.

As expected, the response to Sherman's order was massive and immediate. By June of 1865, 40,000 freedmen had settled on the confiscated land and had established a self-governing community led by Baptist minister Ulysses Houston, a member of the group that had originally met with Sherman to conceive the idea for the land transfer. Although Sherman's original order spoke only of land transfer, the general now ruled that the army could lend mules to the new settlers.

To the shock, surprise, and dismay of not only the settlers, but of freedmen and supporters of abolition throughout the nation, Andrew Johnson overturned the land transfer order in the Fall of 1865, thereby displacing the settlers and returning the land to the same former slavers that had ceded from the Union, formed the Confederacy, and declared war on the United States.

Furious at how President Johnson had allowed Southern states to pass Black Codes and elect former Confederates to the House of Representatives, Congress passed the Civil Rights Act of 1866 which defined citizenship and affirmed that all citizens were equally protected by the law. Intended to support the Thirteenth Amendment, the bills were twice vetoed by President Johnson, but a two-thirds majority in each congressional chamber overrode the veto. Between 1866 and 1867, Congress would pass four Reconstruction Acts which defined requirements for Southern states to be readmitted to the Union.

The Fourteenth Amendment, adopted in 1868, provided citizenship and equal protection under the law for all citizens. The Fifteenth Amendment, passed two years later, completed Reconstruction legislation by finally granting all black men the right to vote. Shortly before its passage, black men had gained the right to vote in the District of Columbia despite a presidential veto that was overridden by Congress.

Between 1870 and 1871, Congress also passed three Enforcement Acts, criminal codes intended to add teeth to the three new amendments. The first act established penalties for interfering with a person's right to vote and gave federal courts enforcement power. The second act permitted federal oversight of local and state elections. The third, and perhaps the most important, became known as the Ku Klux Klan Act. It made state officials liable in federal court for depriving anyone of their civil rights. It further labelled many Klan intimidation tactics as federal offenses and authorized the president to call out the militia to suppress such activities. Finally, it prohibited those suspected of conspiracy against the government from serving on juries related to the Klan's activities, and it authorized suspension of habeas corpus as necessary to control Klan violence.

Upon enactment of the Klan Act, federal troops, rather than state militias, were used to enforce the law, and Klansmen were prosecuted in federal court where juries now included blacks. As a result, hundreds of Klan members were fined or imprisoned, and habeas corpus was frequently suspended in Southern jurisdictions. With continuing pressure from the Klan Act and other Enforcement tools, it appeared to many that the Klan would soon be driven into submission.

While many celebrated the situation, the Klan was nowhere near dead. Even though it would not return to full strength for many decades, anti-black sentiments still abounded among former Klan members. Former Confederate states were often reluctant to punish or take extreme actions against Klansmen, as many local and federal politicians were either former members or lacked the courage and commitment to fight the hate group.

Chastened by their earlier Grand Lodge rebuke for implying Masonic support of their pushback against Black Codes, Solomon and his Frater group avoided inference of Masonic support or involvement in any of their future initiatives. But they did not waver in their belief that black Americans and the nation itself faced great danger with the postwar resurgence of white supremacy and the attack on civil rights. Few groups, they believed, were better positioned to observe the national backsliding than Prince Hall Masonry, its membership permeating so many aspects of American culture. As the Fraters saw it, since Masons were free men, nothing should prevent them from networking among themselves to advocate for any issue they supported as long as that issue did run counter to Masonic principles or goals.

To the Fraters, the failure of Masons to address any of the many human rights challenges still facing the nation could be considered dereliction of their obligation to lead productive lives and serve their communities. At an informal dinner gathering following a lodge meeting in the Fall of 1873, the Fraters lamented what seemed to be a nationwide retreat from the goals of Reconstruction. They discussed actions that Masons might take to prevent further erosion of the hard-won gains of the Civil War. But they wondered whether there was anything that could be accomplished without formal Masonic approval.

Amos Jackson, one of Solomon's co-conductors in the Eliza Cobbins escape, took no issue with independent action, but wondered aloud whether the Ku Klux Klan Act or any other legislation could possibly eliminate Southern white terrorism and preserve the gains of Reconstruction. If not, he asked, what could be done and what role, if any, should Masons play?

"As I see it, the Klan and all the slavers have finally been put down," opined Roscoe Wilkens. "With the Klan Act now in force and the Constitution amended, shouldn't we just give the fixes a chance to work? I'm looking forward to my first opportunity to vote. I hope it comes soon."

"Are you serious?" Amos fired back. "We can never relax until the last Negro has actually voted. Hope for something in the future should have nothing to do with it! We fought hard to gain that right, and we should be able to exercise it right now, with no further delays.

"But these crackers still have a few tricks up their sleeves," he continued. "There are still enough Klan sympathizers embedded in state and federal bureaus to block our vote by failing to enforce new legislation.

Hell, they might even enact new laws that take away other rights we've already earned."

"Voting is important," interrupted Ralph Dawkins. "But that ain't all there is to it," added the grizzled Civil War veteran who fiercely supported Frater activities, but rarely spoke up. "My sister in Georgia tells me about how the first Republican governor got elected back in in 1868. She tells me that everyone knew it was the Negro vote that got him in office because before we could vote, the governor had always been a Democrat. But in that same election, three duly elected colored state senators and twenty-nine colored state representatives were prevented from taking office because the legislature claimed that the state constitution made no provision for Negro legislators."

"So, we got the vote," Ralph continued, slamming his fist on the dinner table so hard that uncleared plates rattled. "But what good does that do if we can't take the office?

"And even though we've finally gotten the right to vote, there's lots of places we better not even think about exercising that right! All those old slavecatchers and out-of-work former reb' soldiers now spend their time terrorizing colored folks to prevent us from voting, living in certain parts of town, or trying to get jobs they don't want us to have. They form all these hate groups: The Klan, The Pale Faces, The White League, and so many others, I can't keep up with 'em.

"Nobody is going to stop these fanatics. Too many public offices, not just in the South, are now held by former Confederate generals pardoned by Johnson." Thumbing through one of the small pocket Constitutions that the Fraters had recently been passing out at community association meetings," the old soldier asked: "How in the Hell can that be? I never did read real well but even I can see right here in Part Three of the Fourteenth Amendment that these people are breaking their own laws."

The group listened patiently as Ralph began reading laboriously:

No person shall be a Senator or Representative in Congress, or elector of President and Vice President or hold any office, civil or military, under the United States, or under any State, who, having previously taken an oath, as a member of Congress, or as an officer of the United States, or as a member of any State legislature, or as an executive or judicial officer of any State, to support the Constitution of the United States, shall have engaged in insurrection or rebellion against the same, or given aid to the enemies thereof.

Closing his Constitution, Ralph offered his final comments in a voice dripping with sarcasm. "And all the old planters are once again sittin' pretty. They jumped on Johnson's amnesty plan and reclaimed all the land that had been taken from them and turned over to freedmen under the Confiscation Act. Long gone are any dreams of forty acres and a mule."

"You guys are dead right," Solomon added, standing and gesturing as he spoke. "This wouldn't be the first time we've seen what looks like progress, only to have the rug pulled out from under us when we let down our guard. A lot of white folks all over this country don't have a pot to piss in, but they've been convinced that it's not white power brokers that keep them broke and in menial dead-end jobs, but that the black man is their real enemy! It's a sad situation.

"It's already been eight years since we won the Civil War and thought we crushed the Confederacy. But thanks to Andrew Johnson and others like him, few of the traitors and secessionists have been punished. Instead, they've come right back with Black Codes. We may think we're solving problems, but every time we take a step forward, they push us back two, and most of America isn't noticing or doesn't care! The country is relieved that the war is over and is no longer even thinking about making amends for all the pain caused by the curse of slavery.

"Forget about any reparations," Solomon continued impatiently. "Killing the Forty Acres and a Mule initiative was the first of Johnson's mischief when he took the presidency. In a quick minute, he took away land occupied by 40,000 freed slaves.

"The closest that citizens of color will ever come to reparations has already happened and it was an accident! On April 16, 1862, eight months before his Emancipation Proclamation, Lincoln signed The District of Columbia Emancipation Act which freed the entire enslaved population here in the District. Unlike the Proclamation, which would not reimburse slavers for releasing slaves, the DC legislation paid up to $300 for each slave freed by owners who remained loyal to the Union. The initiative was intended to reimburse white slavers for the loss of their free labor, thereby ensuring their continued loyalty to the Union cause.

"According to a report I saw in Treasury, some 1,000 slave owners filed petitions to be reimbursed for approximately 3,000 slaves they released. But unexpectedly, a handful of the petitions were filed by black people," Solomon added, the frown momentarily gone from his face. "One of them, Gabriel Coakley, was himself formerly enslaved. An industrious man, Coakley had earned and saved enough to purchase his own freedom. He went on to purchase his wife, his sister, and all his six of his children. Wisely, he retained ownership of all eight, thereby protecting them from such anti-freedmen initiatives as mandatory colonization. Coakley 'freed' his family when his petition was approved, and he was paid for their 'release.'"

Solomon paused momentarily as he scanned the faces of the six Fraters before him. Three of them, like him, had been born free, two had escaped slavery, and one had bought his own freedom. His voice had begun to crack as he attempted to calmly describe the cruel irony of the pittance inadvertently paid to a handful of human bondage survivors through a program not intended to assist and uplift them as victims of generations of injustice, but to compensate oppressors who had lost their long-held privileges of enslaving and abusing others.

After an impromptu round of 'Amens' and expressions of shock and disapproval from the Fraters, Solomon continued, his brow once again knitted. "Because of my work in the Treasury Department, I'm privy to a lot of information about Reconstruction and how it's supposed to be reenergizing our democracy. What I'm seeing and hearing is very scary.

"Johnson was rightly run out of office after his impeachment, but Grant isn't much better. He was a good wartime general, but he's a weak, scandal-ridden president who's afraid to use the army to bring justice to the South, prevent future insurgencies, and hold the former Confederacy accountable for its treason. The Klan Act empowered him to use federal troops to enforce the Civil Rights Act, but the army that numbered a million during the war has shrunk to only 30,000. And only 4,300 soldiers are currently on duty in Southern posts. There's no way an occupying force that small could watch over 750,000 square miles and the nine million people who live in the South.

"Even if enough troops were available," Solomon added, "it's doubtful that Congress would be willing to foot the bill for an occupying army, considering the heavy debt hanging over our heads from the war we supposedly just won. This is a serious problem, as in the next election, Democrats will likely sweep both houses of Congress and probably the presidency. They have already been complaining about the threat of 'military rule.' So, if they get back to power, they will likely ban *Posse Comitatus*, which would prevent the use of the army to address domestic crises. That would be the height of hypocrisy considering their earlier use of the same mechanism to retrieve fugitive slaves."

"The situation sounds bad. A lot worse than I thought," Amos responded. "But what can we do? I think you're right that we should be able to take independent action as individual Masons. But what kind of help could we provide, individually or collectively?"

With several others nodding in support of Amos's unreadiness, Solomon responded. "We've got to be realistic. The problem is huge, and there's only so much we could possibly accomplish. But one thing we can do is shed light on this situation and perhaps help awaken the public to the nation's backsliding and continued failure to live up to its lofty constitutional goals of equality and basic human rights for all.

Raising the national consciousness and commitment to fair treatment of freedmen is not only the right thing to do, but it continues the work of the fallen president who fought so hard for our freedom.

"Most of the public still doesn't understand or accept how America's original sin of slavery was such a serious violation of its own Constitution. This lack of awareness is especially troublesome since, at its founding, the nation had just fought a war to escape European tyranny and repression. But only ninety years later, after fighting yet another war and struggling through a failing Reconstruction, the US is still failing to live up to its constitution.

"I've heard it said," Solomon added, "that the past is prologue. That certainly seems to be true here in America right now. In a hundred years, will our descendants still be fighting for the same human rights? In 1973, will America still be struggling to pass civil rights legislation and a voting rights act?

"As Prince Hall Freemasons, perhaps we can shed light on America's predicament and how, after winning the Civil War, the nation is still failing its citizens of color. A national awareness of the situation is no guarantee that improvement will come, but failure to recognize the problem ensures that improvement will never come.

"Members of our order are embedded in all aspects of the American culture and workplace," Solomon concluded. "And to most of the public, our Masonic identity is usually unknown. Thus, we are well positioned to function, unobtrusively, as human rights violation sensors. Armed with the right information, we can mount public-awareness campaigns to prick the American conscience and prod political and community leaders to act. We already know that progressive newspapers like the *National Republican* would be anxious to report our findings. I'm sure Frederick Douglass would be eager to report on them in *New Era*, the tabloid he's about to launch. I would rather he sound the alarm on the failure of Reconstruction than criticize us as he has done recently. I read where he claimed that Prince Hall Masonry '...is swallowing up the best energies of many of our best men, contenting them with the glittering follies of artificial display, and indisposing them to seek for solid and important realities.'"

With all present murmuring their amens, Roscoe responded. "So, if I'm hearing you brothers correctly, we will be calling on well-placed information sources in the Masonic network to provide us with insights into white supremacist conspiracies to roll back new constitutional amendments and eliminate their enforcement. That information will then be used in a campaign to call public attention to the sabotage of Reconstruction. I'm in agreement, but I'm wondering if it's realistic to try to pull this off with just a handful of Fraters?"

"It would be great if we got our own lodge involved," Solomon answered. "If I continue progressing through the chairs, I'll soon reach the East, and as master of the lodge, I'll try to make that happen. But all that will take precious time that we don't have. The way I see it, a public awareness program on the dangers of allowing Reconstruction to be killed is too important to be put on hold for any reason. We have no way of knowing whether our efforts will open any eyes or inspire people to fight back. But we've got no choice. We've got to shed some light on an insurrection that's going on right under our noses! Hopefully, the same kind of planning is going on in other lodges."

"I say we move ahead immediately," Amos responded. "Look at it this way: as Americans, we don't have to get approval from the government to speak out as concerned citizens. The same is true for our church or political party affiliation. So why do we need approval to be able to speak out on important issues as concerned Masons? It would be nice if we could get our whole lodge involved. Even better would be Grand Lodge support. But I propose that we proceed with or without lodge involvement or Grand Lodge support."

After additional comments by Amos, Solomon and others, the group resolved to launch its campaign. They elected to begin by reporting on Reconstruction rollback activities in Washington DC. Because of his city government position, Solomon was asked to lead the initial effort. Based on the results achieved locally, efforts might be expanded to other locations.

———————————⚬———————————

Using his Treasury, War Department, and congressional contacts, Solomon and his team begin by reviewing postwar events, both government actions and behind-the-scenes maneuvering that had moved the District from a biracial, voting democracy to total disfranchisement. Republicans had swept the 1869 local elections, and black men were securing city government positions in record numbers. The 1870 passage of the Fifteenth Amendment had brought out large numbers of black voters in Washington and other cities throughout the nation. Black Washingtonians had begun to organize politically and mobilize in support of issues relevant to their community. But angry conservative Democrats and white supremacists denounced the changes. Unable to escape the provisions of the Fifteenth amendment, Conservatives attempted to create other barriers to black suffrage. Wealthy businessmen promoted the notion that because of their long-standing investment in their communities, property owners alone should have the right to select local political leaders. They argued that allowing the poor to rule empowered them to unfairly tax and spend other people's money.

The death blow for DC voting rights came in the form of a movement to consolidate Washington City, Washington County, and Georgetown, the District's three separate governmental units, into a single administrative body not controlled by voters but by an unelected board of commissioners appointed by the president. Promoters of consolidation justified it as a path to more efficient and cost-effective city government. They argued that the three separate jurisdictions caused confusion, delayed important development projects, and resulted in excessive, duplicate costs. They contended that consolidation was a business necessity unrelated to politics or Negro suffrage.

Despite the effort to package consolidation as a race-neutral initiative aimed at improving government efficiency and cost-effectiveness, government insiders knew that there were other motivations for the change. Consolidation's undemocratic approach and the ultra-conservative composition of its supporters made it clear that the real motivation behind the proposed change was to control black political power, reduce taxation and spending, and eliminate the corruption most white conservatives believed would result from black suffrage.

The consolidation movement gained momentum when it was endorsed by the conservative-leaning *Evening Star*, a local newspaper which argued that granting citizens the right to vote had been a fool's errand that empowered ignorant former slaves to interfere with good governance, causing the District to lose substantial benefits that might have been gained under an administration controlled by the federal government.

But the concept of sacrificing the right to vote for increased federal funding prompted outrage in the black community and among progressive Republicans. An 1868 proposed amendment to the city charter to replace the elected municipal government with a federally appointed commission was blasted by the city council as an attempt to disfranchise freedmen and have them governed by a moneyed aristocracy.

Addressing church groups and community organizations, the Fraters set out to mobilize public opinion against the changes. They joined irate District residents in sending petitions and complaint letters to Congress. The public outrage and pushback proved effective, at least for the moment. A Congress that was still under Republican control voted to renew the city's charter with no changes to its government structure or the voting rights of its citizens.

But things did not go well under the subsequent election of Mayor Sayles Bowen, an outspoken supporter of emancipation and racial integration. The progressive coalition that elected Bowen in 1868 quickly splintered as a result of administrative missteps and budget problems. The *Evening Star* joined the criticism accusing Bowen of ruling the District with contempt for the colored population, manipulating them to support wasteful and ill-conceived policies.

The inept Bowen administration lasted only one term and breathed life back into the consolidation movement, its supporters claiming that Negro voters had exercised their franchise poorly. To ensure that no such mistakes would ever again be made, they lobbied Congress to create a single territorial government for a consolidated District of Columbia. The effort proved effective, and in 1871, Congress established a new administrative unit consisting of a presidentially appointed governor and Legislative Council together with a popularly elected house of delegates and a non-voting representative in the US House of Representatives.

The Fraters once again joined with the black community in protesting the new territorial government. Public opinion was overwhelmingly against disfranchisement, and many public workers went on strike. But the voice of protest was somewhat muted with the selection of influential black leaders like Frederick Douglass to fill a third of the territorial government's appointee positions. The appointment of the new DC resident and publisher of *New Era* to the Legislative Council diminished the likelihood that he would editorially attack the new government.

Despite the coopting of so many local leaders, Solomon's team pushed ahead with its public opinion campaign, writing protest letters to congressional leaders and encouraging community groups and labor organizations to do the same. At public gatherings, they provided template letters that citizens could copy to generate their own personal protests.

Territorial government failed as badly as the Bowen Administration it replaced. It launched a series of public works projects that beautified the District but created unmanageable debt. The new government's collapse was aggravated by the Panic of 1873, a financial crisis that wreaked havoc in the US banking system causing the failure of many banks. An 1874 Congressional investigation into the territorial government concept exposed evidence of serious mismanagement and graft. Congress immediately voted to end Territorial Government and transfer management of the city to a board of three presidentially appointed commissioners.

Disfranchisement in the District of Columbia was now complete. All elements of locally elected municipal government had been eliminated and replaced by a panel of presidential loyalists that had no ties or responsibilities to the community it represented. Strengthened by the imprimatur of the US Congress, the DC disfranchisement bill would be quickly replicated throughout the South.

Stunned but not totally discouraged, the Fraters decided they could best help by documenting the unfortunate sequence of events in an easily digestible pamphlet form that included suggestions for ongoing action. To help maintain public awareness and keep citizens energized to soldier on in the human rights battle, they continued to organize protests, mount letter-writing campaigns and schedule talks to church, community, and labor groups. At each meeting they would provide a copy of their document to each attendee.

But despite these efforts and those of other concerned community members, citizens in the District of Columbia would continue to lose their rights. Similar losses would occur throughout the nation as the relentless attack on Reconstruction gains continued. Although killing voting rights in the three local governmental units within the seat of the national government involved a scheme unique to the District, many other factors would continue to roll back Reconstruction gains throughout the nation.

⸺⸺◦⸺⸺

Reconstruction rollback momentum had begun with the assassination of the president, the recalcitrance of Andrew Johnson to pass needed legislation, the failure of the courts to enforce new laws, and the reluctance of Ulysses Grant to provide necessary resources to enforce compliance. But the movement gained momentum as the scandals of the Grant Administration began to tilt congress from Republican to white Democratic control. This shift ushered in voter restrictions in the form of poll taxes, literacy tests, property ownership requirements, and segregated polling places; changes that helped Democrats consolidate their control. The increased clout of Democrats helped them to create and amplify the Lost Cause image that the Confederacy was not based on slavery but on the South's desire to fight for its dignity and its traditional way of life. A final blow would come with the Compromise of 1877 which removed federal troops from the South, thereby ending Reconstruction once and for all.

One of the most serious setbacks resulting from the death of Reconstruction was the failure of the Freedmen's Savings Bank. Its goal, as bank investor Frederick Douglass had put it, was to instill in the minds of the former slaves "lessons of sobriety, wisdom, and economy, and to show them how to rise in the world."

Solomon was particularly troubled by the unfortunate closure. He had been inspired by the prospect of an institution aimed at helping black people save and accumulate wealth when he read the proposal Congress sent to Treasury for creating the bank. He was proud to have opened his own account as soon as the bank opened its Washington DC branch. The bank opened thirty-seven branches across seventeen states and Washington DC within seven years and collected funds from over 67,000 depositors. At its peak, the Freedman's Savings Bank held assets worth more than $3.7 million.

The concept for the bank had grown out of a January 1865 meeting in which religious, philanthropic, and business leaders gathered in New York to explore the idea of establishing a savings bank for the benefit of new freedmen. This group would include soldiers receiving back pay and bounty payments for enlisting in the service who had no safe place to deposit their money. Also included would be new workers who, lacking experience in managing their own affairs, were either mishandling their pay or being victimized by hustlers. Out of this meeting, a plan was developed to establish a "benevolent" banking institution that would provide Negroes with a secure place to save their money.

The Freedman's Savings Bank would broaden earlier attempts to help the colored soldier to save. A few states had already instituted a system that allowed soldiers to have portions of their pay deducted each month and sent to relatives or held by military officials until the soldiers left the service. In 1864, the Military Savings Bank at Beaufort, South Carolina, was created to secure the deposits of Negro soldiers and civilians. In the same year, two army generals established similar banks in Virginia and Louisiana. Gen. Nathaniel Banks established the "Free Labor Bank," which maintained deposits from thousands of colored soldiers and former slaves. The New York planning group saw these initiatives as temporary measures. They believed a permanent savings bank was needed if Negroes were to make a successful transition from slavery to freedom.

The act signed into law by President Lincoln stipulated that all bank deposits were to be invested in stocks, bonds, Treasury notes, or other securities of the United States. The charter suggested that no loans would be made. It further suggested that "all the assets of the Bank were owned by the depositors in proportion to the deposits of each." A fifty-member board of trustees would manage the bank, and the company's books would be "open for inspection and examination to such persons as Congress would appoint."

Freedman's Bank grew quickly. But despite its promising start, by early 1874, the bank was near default, having been rocked by wide ranging problems including the Panic of 1873, overexpansion, and sadly, mismanagement and fraud. In 1874, in an effort to calm depositors and prevent further runs on its branches, Frederick Douglass was brought in as president. But after depositing $10,000 of his own funds to show his confidence in the enterprise, Douglass came to realize that the bank could not be saved and recommended to Congress that it be closed. On June 29, 1874, Freedman's Bank ceased operation.

The failure of Freedman's Bank was a catastrophic blow to citizens of color throughout the nation. An inspirational dream for wealth building in their communities had been dashed, and many had lost all their savings. Worst of all, contrary to what depositors had been told, the bank's assets were not insured by the federal government. The resulting distrust of the American government and its banking system would linger in the black community for years. For many it would never go away.

Solomon and his team had followed the Freedmen's Bank saga from its earliest days, and most had been depositors. Quickly realizing that nothing could be done to change the disastrous outcome, the group quickly switched its focus from a political perspective to one of human service. Working through all local lodges, they turned their efforts to providing emergency food and shelter services to those who no longer had the funds to provide for themselves. Knowing Masons were expected to respond to such human service emergencies, the Fraters immediately went to work to plan the aid they might be able to provide.

The final nails in the coffin of Reconstruction were the failure to enforce the Civil Rights bill of 1875, the emergence of the Redeemer Movement, and the election of Rutherford Hayes to the presidency in the Corrupt Bargain of 1877. Almost a century would pass before the nation recovered the gains that were won in the Civil war but lost so quickly in the failed Reconstruction.

The last piece of legislation passed during Reconstruction, the 1875 Civil Rights bill, was the first federal public accommodation law passed in the United States. The landmark bill was intended to protect access by all citizens to public accommodations defined as "Inns, public conveyances on land or water, theaters, and other places of public amusement." As expected, the far-reaching bill was widely supported by the black community, but unpopular with most of the remaining public.

Though neither segregationist nor pro-South, Andrew Johnson's successor, Ulysses Grant, did not support the 1875 law and failed to enforce it. Like his predecessor, he was conciliatory to the South and would have preferred softer legislation. His Justice Department ignored the law and never instructed US attorneys to enforce it. In 1881, the Supreme Court would strike down sections of the bill. It would agree that the Equal Protection Clause of the Fourteenth Amendment prohibited discrimination by the state and local government but would disagree that it gave the federal government the power to prohibit discrimination by private individuals and organizations. The Court would also hold that the Thirteenth Amendment was intended to eliminate "the badge of slavery," but not to prohibit racial discrimination in public accommodations.

The dismantling of the 1875 Civil Rights Act was just one component of a wide-ranging and relentless attack on Reconstruction mounted by the Redeemers, a Southern wing of the Democratic party focused on enforcing white supremacy and regaining political power lost at the end of the Civil War. White Southerners chafed under Reconstruction governments in which many Negroes served in elected and appointed positions. Consumed with resentment and the sense of victimization embodied in the Lost Cause myth, former Confederates and plantation owners were unwilling to accept defeat or to live under the domination of Northerners. Impatient with political solutions, Southerners began supporting insurgencies by a variety of paramilitary organizations including a resurgent Ku Klux Klan.

Terrorist bands turned to violence and terrorism to undermine the Republican vote in attacks such as the notorious 1868 Opelousas Massacre in which white terrorists tried to prevent Republicans from winning a St. Landis Parrish election in Louisiana. In the run-up to the election, a teacher at the local Freedman's school was beaten and whipped in front of the children in his class by the local chapter of the Knights of the White Camelia. When local black Republicans threatened reprisals, thousands of Knights were mobilized. They began hunting white and black Republican party leaders, and the next day, lynched the first twenty-seven Negroes captured. Over the next few days, more than two hundred people, in some cases, entire families, were shot and killed. As a result of the attack, no votes were cast in the election, and the local Republican party ceased to function.

The end of Reconstruction was marked by the Compromise of 1877, an agreement between Southern Democrats and Republican presidential candidate Rutherford Hayes to settle the result of the disputed 1876 presidential election. When it became clear that the outcome of the race between Rutherford and Democratic candidate Samuel J. Tilden hinged on disputed election returns from Florida, Louisiana, and South Carolina, Democrats agreed not to block Hayes's election if Republicans withdrew all federal troops from the South. The removal of federal troops meant that even though Republican Hayes held the presidency, Democrats controlled the South, thus enabling them to undo or simply ignore powerful civil rights provisions of the thirteenth, fourteenth, and fifteenth amendments and the associated Enforcement Laws. The sabotage of Reconstruction was now complete.

XX 

Look to The East

The ultimate measure of a man is not where he stands in moments of comfort and convenience, but where he stands at times of challenge and controversy.

Martin Luther King, Jr.

In accordance with Ancient Masonic Charges, Regulations, and Landmarks stipulating that a retiring Worshipful Master must install his successor sometime between his election date, and the subsequent St. John's Day, Solomon was installed as Worshipful Master of Pythagoras Lodge No. 9, Prince Hall Affiliation of Free and Accepted Masons on December 20, 1875. He was particularly pleased and proud that his father, a past master of his own lodge in Ohio had traveled to the District with several of the members of Solomon's Entered Apprentice class to be a part of the first meeting that his son would gavel to order.

After the lodge was opened on the third degree, that of Master Masons, a private ceremony was conducted during which jewels and aprons displayed on a small table near the lodge altar were presented to incoming officers as they were sworn in and requested to recite their obligations. Many of the lodge's upcoming activities would be a continuation of ongoing programs intended to uplift lodge members and serve the community. But as master, Solomon had latitude to propose additional programs he deemed worthwhile for consideration by the craft and the Grand Lodge. In the months leading up to his installation, he had discussed several possible initiatives with the wardens, deacons, and other lodge officers that would take office with him. But the new leadership team faced a daunting challenge finding opportunities to serve in a rapidly deteriorating political and social environment.

The sabotage of Reconstruction had been completed. The impact had been devastating both locally, with disfranchisement in the District of Columbia, and nationally with weak enforcement or outright roll back of hard-won civil rights gains. The inexplicably lenient punishment and tepid conditions of surrender imposed on secessionists had been further relaxed, and terrorist groups like the Klan were openly brutalizing and intimidating blacks who attempted to vote and exercise newly gained rights. Former slavers were back in control of Southern state and local government offices despite a recent revision of the Fourteenth Amendment that barred insurrectionists from holding such positions.

A large anti-suffrage segment of the nation seemed unified in its efforts to force free black workers into an indentured servitude that differed little from their previous conditions of slavery. To add insult to injury, the reversal of Reconstruction gains had been rebranded as an adjustment necessary for efficient and effective government. In Washington, white community leaders and power brokers defended disfranchisement with the claim that local self-government jeopardized the federal government's 50 percent contribution to the city's budget. To this group, budgetary concerns and administrative efficiency were more important than the protection of hard-won political rights.

The mischaracterization of Reconstruction was not limited to Washington. Throughout the nation, public voices lamenting the end of slavery chimed into the notion that emancipation and suffrage were leading to control of government by ignorant Negroes who had no training or understanding of government and the duties of citizenship. In the District of Columbia, the targets of that criticism were working class ex-slaves such as those packed into the alley communities of Solomon's old Foggy Bottom neighborhood. Life was difficult for the mostly poor residents who rented meager dwellings in crime-ridden alleys that had become increasingly segregated as newly freed slaves poured into the city. Alley dwellers were the poor, uneducated, but no-longer docile Negroes who white citizens feared would soon invade their communities.

Despite difficult living conditions, there was a sense of community unity that helped alley residents survive. Families knew each other and cooperated in raising children and protecting the neighborhood. Many became active in Reconstruction-era politics, voting and supporting Republican programs and policies. In recent years they had been led by Perry Carson, a former Union soldier who now served as Washington's single black delegate to the Republican National Committee. In this capacity, he provided disfranchised residents with an opportunity to express concerns within their chosen political party. But his confrontative nature that focused on the racial aspect of every issue repulsed many white delegates opposed to suffrage.

Carson also drew the ire of a local black elite that had emerged during Reconstruction. More educated and polished than their working-class counterparts, this group held prestigious government positions and frowned on behavior that reinforced negative impressions of Negroes and raised questions about their readiness to engage in self-government. One of those most opposed to Carson's boisterous, often disruptive leadership style was Calvin Chase, editor of the city's most prestigious black newspaper, the *Bee*. In passionate editorials, Chase relentlessly attacked the anti-black prejudice of white suffrage-opposers. He argued that the fight against racism should be led by educated Negroes, those he considered true community leaders. Carson and his followers rejected this notion of leadership as elitist favoritism that valued affluent, privileged Negroes more highly their less affluent, grassroots brethren.

Education and affluence were not the only distinguishing factor between the two groups. The elite class had come to define themselves
as mulatto rather than black and had attached prestige to their light-
colored skin and Caucasian-tinged features. It was the same skin-color
stratification Solomon had earlier witnessed within the White House
colored staff. Understandably, black working-class folk resented the
"airs" and condescending attitudes of elites who they believed were not
connected or committed to the broader community of color.

Both Carson and Chase fought the racist roll back of Reconstruction gains with equal passion. Their main difference seemed to be the
question of which segment of the black community was most aggrieved
and best qualified to argue the case. In their ongoing conflict, Chase regularly challenged Carson's leadership position in the RNC delegate selection process. But despite his black press credentials and elite society
connections, Chase was never able to displace his more popular neighborhood adversary.

At the first meeting of Pythagoras Lodge No. 9 in January of 1876, his
first as master, Solomon introduced a new initiative. After completion
of regular lodge business, including review of upcoming degree programs, Solomon addressed the craft.

Brothers, our community is in serious jeopardy as enemies of
emancipation are snatching away hard-won gains of a brutal and
bloody war at a dizzying pace. We are all aware of how much the
progress of Reconstruction has already been reversed. What is
particularly troubling here in Washington is that our community
is not united in fighting this troubling trend. Instead of coordi-
nating our efforts and using a single voice to confront those who

would send us back into slavery, competing segments of the colored community are battling over who can best represent us.

As I see it, it is a fool's errand for the more-affluent among us to be pitted against the less-affluent, or for those who have had the benefit of education to be set against those who have been denied it, and worst of all, for the different skin colorations among us to disparage each other. Nothing good can come of such "crabs in a barrel" interactions. It causes us to lose our focus on the real enemy, those who would continue to take away our rights.

Solomon paused and scanned the brethren to assess their reaction to his message. With all eyes fixed on him and not another sound to be heard in the hall, Solomon continued with added urgency:

No one can be sure that, even with a united voice, we can stop this troubling slide into a new form of slavery. But we can be certain that if continue to fight among ourselves we'll never accomplish anything.

So, brothers, here is my view. As Masons, "we come together on the level and part on the square." Our lodge membership spans all community segments: affluent and less affluent, educated and less educated, dark and light complexioned, and both well-to-do and working-class. Some of us may not like to even acknowledge these distinctions. But since we always come to the lodge as equals and always depart as friends, we don't value any of these segments as better or worse than others. In that spirit, I request that each member of our craft become active in a community or political group that is addressing post-reconstruction and social justice issues. As you involve yourselves in the organization of your choice, I ask that you help to bridge barriers between "competing" subgroups so that, rather than getting bogged down in internal squabbling, the organization can speak in one powerful and united voice.

If every member of the lodge accepts this challenge, we can leverage our collective strength to cross some of the divides in the black community. And if the community is then able to speak loudly and in one voice, we have a good chance of achieving at least some of our social justice goals.

Solomon's proposal was well received by the lodge, and he immediately received many pledges of support from the craft. In the coming months he took the lead in attending as many community meetings and local political forums as his schedule would permit. In subsequent lodge meetings he would repeat his request and invite testimony from the membership.

Although the DC political situation did not improve in subsequent months, it did not further deteriorate. But as Reconstruction governments continued to be overthrown and Ku Klux Klan violence and intimidation increased in other parts of the nation, a steady stream of black migrants flowed into the city. Attracted by such educational institutions as the recently founded Howard University, the District became a magnet for black intellectuals and activists. In time the city's population would become more than one third black. While Solomon and his lodge brothers would never be sure exactly how much their initiative impacted the evolution and growth of the city, they were certain they did no harm.

XXI

Amnesty

I have observed this in my experience of slavery, - that whenever my condition was improved, instead of it increasing my contentment, it only increased my desire to be free, and set me to thinking of plans to gain my freedom. I have found that, to make a contented slave, it is necessary to make a thoughtless one. It is necessary to darken his moral and mental vision, and, as far as possible, to annihilate the power of reason. He must be able to detect no inconsistencies in slavery; he must be made to feel that slavery is right; and he can be brought to that only when he ceased to be a man.

Frederick Douglass

One of Solomon's few regrets in life was the attack he and other members of the St. Lukes Episcopal Church vestry had waged against their pastor, Alexander Crummell, and their efforts to terminate his relationship with the church. An important voice within the abolition movement, Crummell had become Solomon's pastor in 1873 when he was called to serve as rector of St. Mary's Episcopal Mission in Foggy

Bottom. Two years later, Rev. Crummell and the congregation left St. Mary's to found St. Luke's Episcopal Church, the first independent black Episcopal church in the city. They constructed a new church building on upper 15th Street, NW in the Columbia Heights area.

Born in New York and educated at Cambridge University, Crummell lived and worked in Liberia for twenty years where he educated and converted Africans to Christianity. He also appealed, unsuccessfully, for Americans of color to colonize in Africa. Although Crummell was an important and respected voice within the abolition movement, he sometimes met with opposition and resentment from Negroes who misunderstood his programs to uplift people of African descent through economic, social, and political unity. His positive initiatives were sometimes confused with colonization efforts to push the formerly enslaved out of America.

Several members of the St. Luke's congregation and its vestry, Solomon among them, shared ill-conceived animosity for Crummell and many of his outreach efforts. The mistrust was baffling, as Crummell's programs bore no similarity to Lincoln's colonization efforts which had been abandoned many years earlier. With growing mistrust and conflict among the reverend's supporters and his detractors, on March 14, 1882, the St. Lukes Vestry voted, with seven ayes and three nays, to request that the bishop relieve Crummell of his duties as pastor. Solomon was one of the seven who voted to discharge Crummell.

Despite the vestry recommendations, the pastor was not terminated. In the succeeding months, as the anti-Crummell group somehow began to appreciate his good work and outstanding spiritual leadership, earlier concerns and simmering resentments about colonization were forgotten. Crummell would happily serve St. Lukes until his retirement almost two decades later. Troubled by his own earlier misjudgment, Solomon knew that sooner or later, he would have to set things straight with the reverend.

The opportunity came a few months later when Solomon found it necessary to meet with Crummell to discuss an upcoming fundraising initiative. Just before the church finance committee was called to order, Solomon asked Crummell to join him for a moment in an adjoining anteroom.

"Reverend, even though we've moved past the misunderstanding and controversy relating to your missionary work that came to a head last year, I owe you an apology. I wish I could blame my misjudgment of your goals and good work on youthful immaturity, but since I was already thirty-eight and had known you for seven years when I voted against you, that excuse won't work. Quite simply, I was wrong. I and several other members of the vestry jumped to conclusions and cast our votes without a full understanding and appreciation of the issues. Since that time, I like to think I've learned some important lessons about decision making and problem resolution. And I now can recognize the full worth of all that you have done for St. Luke's."

"Mr. Johnson, I appreciate your comments, but no apology is necessary. With your work at the White House and Treasury, I can understand how the concept of colonization resonated differently for you than for me. But I think we're both seeing things a little more clearly, so nothing more need be said other than that I value your friendship and look forward to our continuing church relationship."

"I appreciate your kind remarks as well," Solomon responded, "but the ill will toward you went beyond your advocacy of colonization. Knowing that many crimes against people of color have been committed under the banner of Christianity, members of the St. Lukes congregation were suspicious of your efforts to evangelize in Africa. Their discomfort was fueled by past abuses wrapped in the name of Jesus. Church members are painfully aware that some of the first slaves ever shipped to America in 1562 were chained together under the decks of *Jesus of Lübeck*, a ship commonly known as *The Good Ship Jesus*. I'm sure you are aware of that tragic history. Church members didn't want a pastor who might have attempted to mislead people of color with a false Christianity that could have enabled their enslavement."

"I understand," Crummell quickly responded. "Sadly, the world is full of such misunderstandings. Wars have been waged and entire populations have been persecuted and wiped out over miscommunication and confusion regarding faith and personal freedom. Within your own esteemed Masonic order there is misunderstanding. As we both know, the order teaches a member the duty he owes to God, his neighbor, and himself. It proclaims its foundation is character, its purpose service, and its measure giving. If its mantra is 'Making Good Men Better,' how is it that white Masons here in America refuse to recognize their brethren of color? Isn't their failure and misunderstanding of their own obligation the reason why you Prince Hall Masons had to establish yourselves independently?

"With misunderstanding and intolerance all around us," Crummell continued, "it is our continuing challenge to not get caught up in hysteria and misinformation. It is a daunting challenge, but the way we have overcome misunderstandings and turmoil right here in our own church gives me great optimism that, with the proper motivation, it is possible to overcome injustice and intolerance, not only in church, but throughout society."

"Perhaps so," Solomon responded, "but to be frank, I haven't always shared that perspective. Although I've tried to do my bit in the fight against oppression of our people, I never believed it was possible to eliminate the hateful sense of privilege from the hearts of those who are still trying to enslave us. But I finally came to realize that, in some ways, I have supported that very sense of privilege.

"Because of my military service, my Underground Railroad activities, and Masonic community outreach, I have always thought of myself as a contributing member of society. I'm proud of my Treasury Department accomplishments and how I have built a successful barbering practice. But even though I continue in the fight for emancipation and racial equality, I have also accepted and even embraced segregation. If I'm honest with myself, I must admit that I did so for financial gain. Even worse, when young Fred Woods tried to influence me to soften my position on whites-only barbershop service, I chastised him and told him that any change in the shop's racial policies would hurt the business.

"Barbering has long been a lucrative profession for black men who run a high-end, white's only service. It's a sorry situation, but one that has been passed down to barbers since the days of slavery. We try to reassure ourselves that separating the races doesn't mean we are accepting inequality, but that's not true. It should be obvious that any form of racial segregation in America usually subordinates colored people to white people. If we know that and still accept segregation, we are promoting white privilege. So, by building a barbering business with a whites-only clientele, I and many other black barbers have helped perpetuate the very same false sense of white privilege that we've fought so hard to end. I'm embarrassed that it has taken so long for me to accept this simple reality.

"From here on out, I'm servicing anyone who wants to patronize me," Solomon added, solemnly. "Maybe more folks are ready for change than I suspect. Hopefully so. But if not, I guess that's the unavoidable price of progress."

Recognizing that as Solomon continued to unburden himself, the conversation had become a confessional, Crummell said only: "I understand." His pastoring instinct told him that Solomon had more to say.

"Perhaps because of serious health issues I have recently had to face," Solomon continued, "I have begun to more seriously and critically contemplate the legacy I am establishing. I have come to realize that those of privilege have greater responsibility to work for the public good than to simply serve cautiously, avoid trouble, work hard, and build wealth. I must acknowledge that I enjoy great privilege: a prestigious, trail-blazing government position that grew out of my good fortune to have had access to the president and other government leaders. Yes, I did my bit of military service, and as a younger man, I was all in as an Underground Railroad worker and emancipation partisan. But as I climbed the professional ladder and entered family life, I slowly became more conservative and less of a risk-taker. Of course, some caution is necessary as one's responsibilities grow. But I carried it too far. I regret that I did not sooner appreciate my privilege and more fully meet the attendant responsibilities. I should have fought segregation and the toxic white entitlement it promotes instead of embracing it for personal gain."

After a long pause and a deep breath, Solomon continued. "Though I have always admired fearless and outspoken advocates who demand full and immediate resolution of the injustices faced by people of color in the US, I know that most of us are not cut out for that role. As I have always seen it, worker bees are also necessary to do the people's business quietly and diligently to ensure that governmental and societal systems work efficiently in service of the common man. I have always lived in accordance with that somewhat narrow and conservative view of my duty to my community and my fellow citizens. Perhaps, because of that somewhat restricted perspective, I have not always been able to fully appreciate the contributions of leaders like you who fight for all the right objectives, but who don't always follow the traditional path in doing so. Sometimes it takes a while for people like me to appreciate those brave enough to go against the grain to achieve their goals. It is from that frame of mind that I and other members of the vestry initially reacted so negatively to you and your efforts to colonize in Liberia and convert Africans to Christianity. I'm thankful you were able to withstand the attack and continue your great work.

"Though it may have taken too long, I have resolved many of the conflicts I've described, and rediscovered my community service voice and purpose through Masonic work. As time passed, I began to more fully appreciate and support your innovative programs to uplift both Americans of color and our African brothers. No longer viewing you as a troublemaker who doesn't show proper deference to accepted norms and values, I am now better able to understand your work so that I can help other members of the vestry to also recognize your contributions."

"Brother Johnson, I thank you for sharing these thoughts and insights with me," the reverend responded after pausing long enough to feel comfortable that Solomon had completely unburdened himself. "I appreciate your forthrightness. Many of us do not have the self-awareness and humility necessary to acknowledge shortcomings and recalibrate behavior as you are doing. I'm happier than ever that you are still a part of our vestry. God bless you, my worthy brother. Stay strong."

XXII

Glory

*It's a long old road, but I know I'm gonna find the
end.*

Bessie Smith

In the fourteen years since his first episode of weight loss and coughing, Solomon had been more mindful of his health and fitness. He
had always eaten reasonably well, and after marrying Elizabeth, his diet
improved. Following his doctor's recommendations, he had cut back on
his barbering so that he had more time to relax, exercise, and play with
his children. He hadn't lost any more weight, but he continued to experience night sweats and coughing spells. Now there was a new alarm
bell. The phlegm he had coughed up over the last few days was tinged
with blood. Although he immediately scheduled a doctor's appointment, Solomon didn't need anyone to tell him he was likely afflicted
with consumption.

Still only forty-four and the breadwinner of a young family of seven,
Solomon had long tried to avoid even thinking about such a situation.
In conversations about his health with Elizabeth, the dreaded disease
was never mentioned, and until now, his doctor had never provided a
firm diagnosis.

Only two years earlier in 1882, scientists had determined that consumption was caused by bacteria that attacks the lungs. It had also been learned that the disease was not hereditary, as was previously believed, but in fact was very contagious. Because the bacteria that spread the condition was present in the sputum of those afflicted, a single cough or sneeze might spread thousands of bacteria.

Despite the new awareness of its cause, there was still not yet any reliable treatment or cure for the disease. In the past, physicians had prescribed everything from bleedings and purgings to the ingestion of cod liver oil, but these days, patients were usually advised to rest, eat well, and exercise outdoors. Some doctors now promoted isolation to not only reduce transmission of the disease, but to heal those afflicted. They believed that rest and moderate exercise in cool, fresh mountain air might be a cure. When he learned about the recently opened Adirondack Cottage Sanatorium in Saranac Lake, New York, the first rest home for consumption patients in the United States, Dr. Lawrence suggested that Solomon check in for a one-month recovery stay.

Two days later, Solomon secured a one month leave of absence from his Treasury Department job, and the following morning, he and Elizabeth were seated on a train bound for Saranac Lake, a tiny Adirondack Mountain village in the northeast corner of New York. Planning to remain with Solomon for the first week of his stay, Elizabeth left their children under the care of her parents who would remain in Washington during Solomon's treatment.

After nearly a day-long train ride, Solomon and Elizabeth arrived at their destination, a quaint village high in the Adirondacks. A short carriage ride took the anxious couple to the newly opened sanatorium, which had taken in its first patients only a few months earlier in 1885. Solomon checked into "Little Red," a small cottage that housed the Sanatorium's patients. Elizabeth would stay in a nearby guesthouse.

Adirondack Cottage Sanatorium was operated by a New York City physician who had come to the village nine years earlier to treat his own consumption. With no known treatment at the time, other than rest and nutrition, the disease was usually fatal. But when the dry, fresh air improved his own health, he founded Adirondack Cottage, modelling its design on Alpine European mountain resorts. Convinced that fresh air was key to recovery, he didn't want his patients in a large, institutional setting that exposed them to sanitation problems associated with overcrowding. The treatment he prescribed for Solomon began with complete bed rest and as much fresh air and natural light as possible.

Solomon responded well to the treatment. He loved the setting and the spectacular view from the outdoor terrace on which he spent most of his waking hours. Different from elongated mountain ranges like the Rockies and the Appalachians, the Adirondacks formed a circular dome, one-hundred-sixty miles wide and a mile high. From his elevated perch, Solomon felt as though he could see every one of the many lakes, ponds and forested areas that dotted the region. He particularly enjoyed the many colorful exotic flowers that grew in the area. Surrounding his terrace were two of his favorites, the Dogwood Blossom adorned with greenish white flowers, and the Carolina Spring Beauty a perennial featuring pink and white petalled flowers.

During his first week, Solomon's only activity was to write short letters to a few family members and friends. But, instead of wasting away like many other sanatorium residents, Solomon's coughing episodes became less severe, and he began sleeping more soundly. Ten days after his admission, Solomon began a light exercise program that stimulated his appetite. He was buoyed by the many letters and well wishes received from Elizabeth, his parents, and his children and was particularly touched by unexpected correspondence from Treasury coworkers with whom he had not disclosed the treatment he was to receive or the location where it would be rendered. He had provided only basic information about his treatment to his immediate supervisor. But somehow his coworkers learned the full story and reached out to him.

      Treasury Department
      Third Auditor Office

Washington, D.C.

July 28, 1885

Dear Johnson,

We are all glad to know that you stood the trip to New York so well; and you may rest assured that we hope and pray that the pure mountain air, water, and rest build you up. Take things carefully and make it your business to get well. I shall not trouble you with news about the Division, further than to say that our new chief, Oscar J. Harvey, is on hand and is "taking hold" like a veteran. He is a "tip-top" fellow. He "catches on" and is a gentleman.

The weather is much pleasanter than when you left. Had a big rain Sunday night and yesterday morning. All join in best wishes for your recovery. Aunt Nancy wishes to be specially remembered to you and your wife and wishes she could be up in the mountains with you.

Please write frequently – just a short note to let us know how you are getting along.

Remember me kindly to Mrs. J. and believe me, as ever,

Your friend,
E. D. B. Porter

The outpouring of affection and well-wishes from family, friends, and coworkers lifted Solomon and were a perfect complement to the beautiful and healthful environment. By the end of his one-month stay, Solomon's energy level seemed greater than it had been in many months. Most importantly, he no longer appeared to be coughing blood. Encouraged by the progress, Dr. Lawrence ordered him to be discharged. The following week Solomon was back at work.

Following Dr. Lawrence's recommendations to conserve energy and to not overwork, Solomon returned to his usual office work hours, but eliminated his after-hours barbering and cut back on his Masonic commitments, participating in only the most important activities. The less-strenuous routine allowed him to enjoy family activities with Elizabeth and the children and to engage in moderate outdoor exercise. But two months after his discharge from the sanatorium, Solomon's consumption symptoms returned, now more pronounced than ever. Fatigued so severely that not only was he often unable to work or even get out of bed, he was now also losing weight rapidly.

A pulmonary specialist called in by Dr. Lawrence determined that active consumption bacteria were still causing lesions in Solomon's lungs. It was his opinion that Solomon's lungs needed a rest so that the lesions could heal. A procedure that had recently proved helpful for many patients was to deliberately collapse the lungs, one at a time, by injecting oxygen or nitrogen into the chest cavity and increasing the pressure until the lung collapsed. This course of action not only rested the lung, but killed the bacteria which require oxygen to survive. The collapse wouldn't be permanent, since as soon as gas was no longer pumped into the patient's chest, the lung would once again inflate unless the patient was already in a terminal state.

If it was impossible to utilize the gas injection method, a more invasive and permanent method to collapse the lungs was the removal of ribs in a process called thoracoplasty. By removing the portions of the skeleton which support the chest wall, the lung collapses and is permanently at rest. This extreme approach was considered a last resort, as the complications of such surgery could be disfiguring or even fatal.

After lengthy consultation between the two doctors, it was determined that, in his present state, Solomon's constitution would not tolerate either procedure. In a follow-up meeting with Solomon and Elizabeth, Dr. Lawrence recommended that Solomon undergo a further rest period at home or at the Lake Saranac facility before undergoing either of the lung treatment options.

In the past, Solomon's outlook on life had always been optimistic and forward-thinking. But in the weeks following his most recent setback, he began to contemplate the harsh reality of his mortality; that he would likely never regain his health or live to see his children reach adulthood. Despite the loving attention, the prayers, and words of encouragement from family and friends he received in his now bedridden state, Solomon reached a state of clarity and closure about what lay ahead for him when every member of Pythagoras Lodge appeared unexpectedly at his home one Sunday afternoon.

In full Masonic attire of aprons and white gloves, his fellow members of the craft had come to his home to pray for him. To protect him from unnecessary exposure, they assembled on the front lawn of his home in a large semicircle. When Solomon's bed was wheeled up to a large bay window so that he and his brothers could see each other, they began their prayers for him. It was a solemn, tearful experience that he would never forget. But he couldn't help but break into a broad smile when the brothers concluded their visit with the singing of his favorite spiritual: "Lord, I Don' Done What You Told Me to Do." He wondered how they could have known the piece was so important to him.

Solomon slept well that evening. But a few days later he was gone, called to glory.

The following week, after a warm homegoing service at St. Lukes Episcopal Church, Solomon's family and friends, his pastor, and the members of Pythagoras Lodge stood assembled at the place where he would be interred. Rev. Crummell began with prayer and heartfelt comments describing how he and Solomon had moved beyond a once adversarial and contentious relationship to a place of mutual understanding, respect, and love.

Following the reverend's remarks, Solomon's lodge brothers assembled around his casket for a Masonic Graveside Service, a time-honored ritual that Solomon and past masters of Pythagoras Lodge before him had performed many times for deceased brothers. With the Worshipful Master standing at the east end of the grave, the Senior Warden at the west, the family and other Masons assembled behind the Junior Warden at the south. The Worshipful Master began:

> Brethren, the solemn notes that betoken the dissolution of this earthly tabernacle have again alarmed our outer door, and another spirit has been removed to the land where our fathers have gone before us.... From time immemorial it has been the custom among the Fraternity of Free and Accepted Masons, at the request of a brother, to accompany his remains to the place of interment, and there to deposit them with the usual ceremonies. In conformance with this usage, and at the request of our deceased brother, whose memory we cherish, and whose loss we now deplore, we have assembled in the character of Masons, to offer up his memory before the world, this tribute of our affection, thereby demonstrating the sincerity of our esteem for him, and our steadfast attachment to the principles of Masonry....

The coffin was then lowered into the grave, and Solomon's apron, having been previously removed from his remains, was handed to the master. The master then raised the apron and said:

> The lambskin or white leathern apron is an emblem of innocence and the badge of a Mason, more ancient than the Golden Fleece or Roman Eagle, and when worthily worn, more honorable than the Star and Garter, or any other order. This emblem I now deposit in the grave of our deceased Brother Johnson. By it we are reminded of the purity of life and conduct so essentially necessary

to our gaining ready admission into the Celestial Lodge above, where the Supreme Architect of the Universe presides.

The assembled brothers then jointly presented Grand Honors, a Masonic salute in which each man's arms are crossed on the breast, with the open palms of the hands sharply striking the shoulders; the hands then raised above the head, the palms striking each other, and then made to fall smartly upon the thighs. The sequence was repeated three times, after which the master took off his white gloves. Holding them above his head, he continued:

> This glove is a symbol of fidelity and is emblematic of that Masonic friendship which bound us to him whose tenement of clay now lies before us. It reminds us that while these mortal eyes shall see him not again, yet, by the practice of the tenets of our noble order and a firm faith and steadfast trust in the Supreme Architect, we hope to clasp once more his vanished hand in friendship and in love. Those whom virtue unites; death can never separate.

Following additional comments by the master and a repeat of Grand Honors, the ceremony ended. Solomon was finally at peace.

XXIII

Epilogue

When you know your name, you should hang onto it, for unless it is noted down and remembered, it will die when you do.

Toni Morrison

Solomon James Johnson's years on this earth were few, but his accomplishments were many and his legacy would span more than one hundred years and four more generations of Solomons carrying on both his name and his tradition of black excellence and public service.

His middle son, Solomon, the third of his five children with Elizabeth, strove mightily to live up to the legendary "Sweet" Johnson accomplishments of his father. Born in Washington, DC in 1871, he would attend public elementary schools, the local Minor High School, and go on to matriculate at Howard University. Despite his pharmacy training at Howard, young Solomon would follow his father's footsteps into a career of public service with an initial job as a clerk in the District of Columbia District Attorney's Office. He would follow that assignment with a position in his father's old workplace, the US Treasury Department.

In 1904, he would move to New York City and take a position as an Immigrant Inspector and Interpreter for the US Department of Immigration at Ellis Island. He would remain with Immigration for more than forty years, rising to become the director of the bureau where he would oversee the examination and admission of hundreds of thousands of immigrants into the US from countries all over the world. He would thus continue his father's trailblazing tradition by becoming the one of the first Negro bureau chiefs of a critical government function. In his spare time, he served on the Executive Commission of the Harlem Republican Club and was a member of both the Elks and the Knights of Pythias. On May 31 of the year he came to New York, he married Katherine Du Boyce, a descendant of Kentucky slaves. The pair raised five children, Solomon Jr., Catherine, Charles, Margaret, and Elizabeth.

Born in 1906 and raised in Harlem during the famed Harlem Renaissance of the early 1900s, Solomon "Sol" Jr. would continue to blaze trails and burnish the legacy of a biblical family name that denoted wisdom. After elementary and secondary school in Harlem, he attended Bates College in Maine where he was a star player on the school's varsity football team, an unheard-of accomplishment at the time. He also became an early member of Alpha Phi Alpha, the nation's oldest intercollegiate historically black fraternity. After graduation, Solomon began a career in the performing arts, playing leading man roles in the films of legendary black filmmaker, Oscar Micheaux, his most famous as the character Paul Bronson in the 1937 classic, *Underworld*. Many years later in a rerelease, black actor Brock Peters would introduce the film and cast, and refer to Sol as "our Clark Gable." Following service with the New York National Guard's 369th Infantry, the legendary World War I Harlem Hellfighters, Solomon would manage and co-own a popular Harlem night club with his business partner, William James "Count" Basie.

Since Sol's marriage to Rubie Brodie produced a daughter, but no sons, the task of creating the next Solomon fell to Sol's sister, Margaret (the author's mother, to whom this book is dedicated), and her husband, William Herbert, a Trinidadian immigrant and Harlem Hell-fighter leader who earned his citizenship in the trenches of World War I France. He was also a member of Alpha Phi Alpha as would be men in the next four generations of a hundred-year Alpha family legacy that followed him. In 1939, Solomon Johnson Herbert was born to Margaret and William. This latest Solomon came of age in the turbulent 1960s as African Americans were still fighting to achieve the freedoms promised, but not delivered, in the Declaration of Independence, and won but then lost ninety years later with the death of Reconstruction. Solomon would also serve with the Hellfighters and then as leader of the militant Bronx, NY chapter of CORE, the Congress of Racial Equality. Later he would found the e-magazine Black Meetings and Tourism (BM&T), a travel and business meeting trade journal that he would publish for more than forty years and continues to publish today. Solomon and his wife, Gloria, would raise the next Solomon, their son born in California in 1980. After service as a US Marine, the youngest Solomon would work with his father on BM&T before striking out on his own and trying his hand as an entrepreneur in the trucking industry.

After almost two centuries, the Solomon "Sweet" Johnson legacy continues to unfold, his name carried forward in each of the four generations that followed him. He would be pleased to know that, whether or not named Solomon, his descendants have continued his tradition of leadership and service. Coming generations could not ask for a better template of tenacity, achievement, and excellence.

William G Herbert is a son of the Caribbean. His father a Trinidadian immigrant and his mother a descendant of enslaved African Americans, Herbert was born in Harlem and educated in the public schools of New York City. His military service, university training, and life experience deepened a lifelong interest in black history. He has written three historical novels set within the context of the ongoing struggle for the emancipation and empowerment of people of color in the US and the Caribbean. His most recent book charts the extraordinary life of his own great-grandfather who shared an unusual bond with Abraham Lincoln. Herbert currently resides in Detroit.

For more about Herbert see:
https://williamgherbert.com/